W9-CJT-119

All Together Now

658.4092 Voi

Voisin, G.
All together now.

PRICE: $26.99 (3559/he   )

All Together Now

Vision, Leadership and Wellness

Gail Voisin

DUNDURN
TORONTO

Copyright © Gail Voisin, 2011

The All Together Now Advantage is a trademark with a registered copyright pending.

All rights reserved. No part of this publication may be reproduced, stored in a retrieval system, or transmitted in any form or by any means, electronic, mechanical, photocopying, recording, or otherwise (except for brief passages for purposes of review) without the prior permission of Dundurn Press. Permission to photocopy should be requested from Access Copyright.

Editor: Nicole Chaplin
Design: Courtney Horner
Printer: Marquis

Library and Archives Canada Cataloguing in Publication

Voisin, Gail
    All together now : vision, leadership, and wellness / Gail Voisin.

ISBN 978-1-55488-936-5

1. Executive ability. 2. Leadership.
3. Executives--Health and hygiene. I. Title.

HD38.2.V65 2011   658.4'092   C2010-907738-5

1   2   3   4   5   15   14   13   12   11

We acknowledge the support of the Canada Council for the Arts and the Ontario Arts Council for our publishing program. We also acknowledge the financial support of the Government of Canada through the Canada Book Fund and Livres Canada Books, and the Government of Ontario through the Ontario Book Publishers Tax Credit program, and the Ontario Media Development Corporation.

Care has been taken to trace the ownership of copyright material used in this book. The author and the publisher welcome any information enabling them to rectify any references or credits in subsequent editions.

J. Kirk Howard, President

Printed and bound in Canada.
www.dundurn.com

Dundurn Press	Gazelle Book Services Limited	Dundurn Press
3 Church Street, Suite 500	White Cross Mills	2250 Military Road
Toronto, Ontario, Canada	High Town, Lancaster, England	Tonawanda, NY
M5E 1M2	LA1 4XS	U.S.A. 14150

CONTENTS

FOREWORD

by John C. Marshall

In my role as president of the Self Management Group for over 30 years, I have worked with hundreds of large, successful organizations around the world to help develop self-managed, high-performance cultures. The new globally connected world has presented corporate executives with several unique challenges at both a personal and professional level. Achieving outstanding personal and organizational success in this busy, competitive, exciting world requires a unique, leading-edge set of skills for twenty-first-century executives and leaders.

Over the course of the Self Management Group's work, both in North America and around the globe, we have worked with a multitude of organizational development experts, facilitators, and executive coaches. Gail Voisin has distinguished herself by combining her refreshing, stimulating, and engaging personality with an integrated approach based on solid academic theory and proven through many years of refinement as a successful practitioner. As a pioneer in the 1980s, she was one of the first organizational development specialists in Canada to design and incorporate health and wellness into core management/ leadership development programs. Gail was also one of the first to recognize that a leader needed to develop a healthy lifestyle by incorporating stress management and fitness in order to have the ability and energy to grow a successful organization. This integrated perspective was initially viewed with skepticism, and definitely not considered mainstream.

Maintaining the energy to continue developing her approach required an integrated commitment and expertise in the three areas of vision, leadership, and wellness. I believe Gail has an integrated solution unlike anyone else in the world to date. I've worked closely with her and have personally witnessed the results of her executive coaching with many client organizations over the last two decades. I know she has a value-add approach that works, because I have seen the outstanding results achieved with her clients. This book is about the profound power of integrating vision, leadership, and wellness to achieve extraordinary success — her compelling brand: The All Together Now Advantage.

It does not matter *how* a corporate executive aligns vision, leadership, and wellness until they truly understand *why*. That's what this book is about. It will help you understand the heart of vision, leadership, and wellness in ways you may never have considered before. Using her experience from her work with hundreds of corporate executives as a guide for success, Gail has condensed the insights of hundreds of books on these topics. By incorporating the key information related to vision, leadership, and wellness into an integrated solution, this book will be your guide to maximizing your performance and achieving a healthy, balanced life.

Gail is a world-class coach, educator, and expert on leadership development, lifestyle management, succession planning, and strategic business planning. She continually collaborates with world experts to ensure that her methods are leading edge. Gail is committed to exceptionally high standards of excellence, and this book is no exception. As one of corporate America's most highly trusted executive coaches, one of Gail's natural gifts is her outstanding ability to build trust and rapport in her relationships with corporate executives and client organizations. She is greatly respected for her honest and candid feedback to clients, and is known for "calling it like it is!"

By reading this book, you will learn about real life situations where Gail's expert coaching has made a real difference in the quality of the lives of many corporate executives. Her enthusiasm is contagious and her success is inspirational.

All Together Now is a must read for today's corporate executives. Most of us have perceived vision, leadership, and wellness as important, but separate areas. However, this book demonstrates the importance of integrating all three, and provides a template for balancing all three as important daily commitments. Gail's ongoing executive coaching work and the information in this book demonstrate that it is the *integration* that makes such a huge difference to the quality of your personal and professional work, health, and lifestyle.

She also integrates and links the three areas — vision, leadership, and wellness — with the strategic business plan of the particular organization to measure and report on the return on investment of the coaching work. She's an expert in working with corporate executives to ensure that succession planning is directly linked to their strategic business plan for the ongoing momentum of retaining and attracting top talent for the short and long term profitability of the organization.

Today's global corporate world is fast-paced and competitive. Executives who master the *integration* of vision, leadership, and wellness will not only be in high demand by the world's most progressive and successful organizations, they will also be the executives who sustain peak performance, while maintaining a balanced and high-quality personal life. The rewards are exceptional. Aligning vision, leadership, and wellness is the foundation to living the life of your dreams.

As you proceed through this book, you will not only enjoy Gail's unique perspective, but you will also develop an appreciation of Gail's unique character and the energy devoted to helping others enjoy success, health, and happiness.

John C. Marshall, Ph.D.
Toronto, Canada

AUTHOR'S NOTE

The examples, anecdotes, and characters in this book are drawn from my executive leadership development and lifestyle management and consulting work with real people and live interventions. As a result, names and some identifying features and details have been changed.

This book is based on my experiences, relationships, interviews, and observations over the last two and a half decades, having worked as a corporate executive in leadership development and wellness in five different industries, as well as founding my own executive leadership development and lifestyle management practice 15 years ago.

This book will significantly increase your knowledge of the importance of aligning vision, leadership, and wellness to achieve extraordinary success, but at no time should you rely solely on this book to resolve your coaching problems. Each individual is unique with a different set of specific needs and what works for them. Although this book includes general information relating to health, legal, and financial areas, it does not offer advice that is customized to your needs and should not be used for that purpose. To get help with your unique needs and objectives, you should consult a competent professional with particular expertise in that specific area. This book is intended to work as the foundation, taking you to the next step in your professional development.

A powerful engine, weighing hundreds of tons, keeps the ship moving, but it's the needle of a compass — weighing just a fraction of an ounce — that keeps the ship on course.

INTRODUCTION

Excellence is not an act; it is a habit.

— *Aristotle*

I cannot teach anybody anything; I can only make them think.

— *Socrates*

This book is about the importance of aligning vision, leadership, and wellness to achieve extraordinary success.

It is quite possible to be a high performer, maximize your skills and potential, and have a balance of wellness in your life. I call it "having a life!" Since we are on this planet only once, I believe each one of us deserves to have that great life now.

For most corporate executives, every day is a constant challenge to balance the many facets of life — careers, family and friends, health, and personal goals. Where one element is successful and fulfilled, more often than not, another is straining. The pace of life today, and the technologies that support it, create a blur between the home and the office. There is often no real distinction. It just is. The purpose of this book is to inspire you to understand that it does not have to be a daily struggle. For when you understand the importance of integrating your personal and organizational vision, leadership, and wellness, you will have the foundation to achieve extraordinary success in your personal and work life.

As an executive coach over the past two and a half decades, I feel honoured and privileged to have worked both one-on-one and in groups with some of the brightest minds and most brilliant executives in corporate America in a variety of industries. Over the years, I have developed a method which has since become a compelling brand called The All Together Now Advantage The diagram below illustrates this model.

Total Balance and Integration Model

The All Together Now Advantage makes the case that by aligning vision, leadership, and wellness, both personally and organizationally, you naturally position yourself to achieve extraordinary success. You will achieve greater results while expending less energy. You also become more resilient for meeting future challenges. When understood and practised with commitment, The All Together Now Advantage has had profound results for the hundreds of corporate executives I have coached. I believe it can do the same for you.

All Together Now is about the importance of integrating the key areas of vision, leadership, and wellness under one umbrella to achieve extraordinary success in both your business life and personal life. It demonstrates that when executives align their personal and organizational vision with their leadership ability and wellness, they can live the life of their dreams.

WHY DID THIS BOOK NEED TO BE WRITTEN?

The world is full of people who call themselves coaches. In fact, we may have lost sight of the true meaning of the word. In my view, an authentic coach needs to look at the individual from a whole-person perspective — personally and professionally — in terms of the three key areas of vision, leadership, and wellness. Just as a successful organization needs to be healthy and resilient to sustain long-term performance results, so do individual executive leaders. A coach can inspire their clients to achieve personal and professional excellence and fulfillment in these areas.

The seeds for this book were planted over 20 years ago. In the 1980s, while working in the consumer packaged goods industry, I was one of the first corporate organization development specialists in Canada to design and incorporate health and wellness into core management/leadership development programs. I led the way in breaking new ground in corporations by introducing and linking key aspects of stress management and fitness to productivity and profit.

There were skeptics. In fact, at the time, some corporate executives laughed at me as though I was from outer space. Fortunately, with my dedication, the leading edge corporate executives did come to support my direction on fitness and wellness. They became convinced that the corporate world really had to change to include broader aspects of health in order to be competitive, to attract top talent, and to sustain performance. My clients are proof that true extraordinary success for executives comes from mastering the areas of vision, leadership, and wellness.

As my career moved on to other industries such as high tech, sports broadcasting, and retail, I noticed a distinct pattern. Where there was a supportive environment for an employee's fitness and work/life balance, there was ongoing productivity and high achievement levels. Where there was a lack of support, there was major burnout, high turnover, and loss of productivity and profits for the organization. Back then, it was difficult to get the attention of the CEO on matters related to work/life balance without proof of results. However, today there are tangible ways to measure these results. This shows how far we have come.

In my coaching practice, I work with corporate executives to integrate and link vision, leadership, and wellness into their strategic business plans so they can measure and report on return on investment for the organization. The executive clients I have coached tell me that the combination of services I provide is unique. Though some coaches may have expertise in organizational behaviour, others in leadership, and others experts in lifestyle management or wellness, my uniqueness is to combine in-depth expertise in all three areas. We all know how valuable time is to any executive, so the advantage of working with one expert to gain insight into all three areas has been a definite benefit for my clients. It was the consistent feedback, as well as requests and encouragement from my clients to write a book to further inspire them to be better people and better leaders, that grew into the book you are holding.

The work in my coaching practice keeps me informed of the many theories of organizational development and leadership. I translate these complex theories into practical, hands-on skills and knowledge for my clients. My colleagues and friends know that I read about 150 books a year on topics including business, finance, psychology, leadership, and wellness. Although there are plenty of outstanding books written separately on topics of leadership, wellness, and vision, none that I have discovered to date incorporate all three topics. More importantly, none *integrate* all three topics. However, my extensive coaching experience tells me that it is the *integration* that executives really need to understand in order to achieve extraordinary success. Inspiring you on the importance of aligning and integrating vision, leadership, and wellness is the main reason I wrote this book.

I want to share with you the best of what I have learned through my studies and my real life experience about what works for corporate executives. This solid foundation of work links back to the wisdom of philosophers like Socrates and Aristotle. The concepts are simple yet powerful. With this book, I've tried to meet the specific challenges faced by corporate executives who experience ongoing demand for peak performance in organizations while wanting to maintain a balance of wellness in their life.

My sincere hope is that this book will ignite some of your own thoughts about living a more meaningful, gratifying, healthy, and purpose-driven life, while at the same time achieving your personal and corporate dreams.

ALIGNING VISION, LEADERSHIP, AND WELLNESS TO ACHIEVE EXTRAORDINARY SUCCESS

For corporations to be successful, they must have leaders who can thrive in the fast pace of business and life in the twenty-first century. Their focus is on profit and integrity, honesty, and trustworthiness. Those who do it well are the leaders who help create compassionate organizations while sustaining profitability. Organizations need to retain and develop those leaders to grow their organizations. Leaders who do not understand the need to master the integration of vision, leadership, and wellness will be at a disadvantage when it comes to thriving in the marketplace, as well as in their ability to develop others.

Allow me to briefly explain what I mean by vision, leadership, and wellness. Vision is the ability to develop a compelling overall goal or direction that matches your personal belief or value system. That compelling goal becomes a purpose or mission in business, your personal life, or both. Your vision needs to be so clear and laser-focused that it is apparent that your passion has been ignited whenever articulating and communicating it to others. Your vision is supported by your values. We use our values to evaluate possible courses of action, what is and what is not acceptable. Living our values ensures that we have personal and organizational integrity, credibility, and authenticity.

Leadership is the ability to inspire others to willingly adopt a specific viewpoint or course of action as their own, to the extent that they are highly committed to the course of action because they find personal fulfillment in accomplishing the results. Leadership also means providing direction to staff and the organization in applying the skill sets that best maximize productivity and best tap into the talent of the individuals for overall profitability for the stakeholders. To thrive in the twenty-first century, a high level of self-awareness and an understanding of how your behaviour impacts others are key to mastering the fundamentals of leadership. Exceptional leadership includes being committed to doing what you say you will do, being trusted, being authentic, fostering a learning and growth environment for others, and being a strong role model. Each of these has a ripple effect on all levels of staff in the organization.

Wellness and lifestyle management means maintaining a healthy mind and body, and having a reserve of energy to access when required. This helps you meet any exceptional needs and circumstances beyond your control in business and family life. Ideally, you want to be able to sustain optimal performance by ensuring that the time out for re-energizing occurs when required, to avoid burn-out from ever happening.

All three elements — vision, leadership, and wellness — must be integrated in order to achieve extraordinary success. And yet, though I have met many executives who excel in one or two areas, rare is the executive who has experienced the power of the integration of all three.

Integrating
Vision, Leadership, and Wellness

Vision and leadership, without wellness

Imagine, for example, an executive who is strong in vision and leadership, but lacks wellness. These executives do not have the emotional and physical energy or stamina to sustain long-term performance. They may have a tremendous desire to develop a vision and execute that vision through leadership, but the physical and mental performance of the body is not being nourished to withstand the ongoing stresses experienced by most executives.

Perhaps you have met someone like Tim, a forward-thinking business leader whose life is out of balance. Tim is passionate about his personal vision, which is aligned to his organization's vision. He leads his organization to achieve outstanding profits and provides an incredible return on investment for shareholders in the short term. He is respected and admired. His boss, the senior vice-president of marketing, shared with me that Tim was one of the best strategic visionaries on his executive team and was one of their best leaders in the past. However, recently he wasn't demonstrating his usual passion for the job, or being an inspiring leader to his team.

When I met Tim, he had been divorced for two years, and was a single parent sharing custody of two young boys. As we started our coaching relationship, discussing the wellness dimension of his life, Tim told me that he had been working longer hours over the past few years and had gradually gained about 10 pounds. He also shared with me that he was shocked to discover at his recent annual physical that his blood pressure was too high and his LDL cholesterol was above normal, and that, for the first time ever, he had to take medication to solve these problems. Over the course of Tim's coaching, he began to take more ownership of his wellness. I helped connect him with a nutritionist. Within three months, Tim was starting to feel much better. By being more disciplined about his food choices and committing to regular exercise, as well as trying yoga and meditation for the first time, Tim lost eight pounds within six months. More than that, he was able to get off his blood pressure medication. With his newfound knowledge of nutrition, Tim and his two boys often have fun cooking healthy meals together on the weekend. Feeling better physically made Tim more energetic and confident. He's maintaining a healthy mind and body, has a reserve of resilience, and is back to achieving extraordinary success and peak performance in his organization.

Leadership and wellness, without vision

What if you are an executive who has leadership and wellness, but lacks vision? These executives are missing a compelling direction for themselves and others to adopt and pursue. They are running aimlessly in circles; definitely busy, but not clearly going anywhere.

Consider Cathy, an executive with a degree of direction for the short term with some basic objectives. However, she did not have any deeply established focus, purpose, or direction for the long term. Cathy was frustrated and had difficulty staying motivated because she couldn't sustain that "good feeling," the euphoria that comes with a solid purpose. She did not see the long-term vision for the organization, her role, or herself. There was nothing to ignite her passion or to sustain her desire to build and grow herself, her team, or the organization. Vision is the underlying link that naturally energizes, motivates, and excites our reason for being and doing. Yet, Cathy hadn't discovered, clarified, or articulated her vision.

When I first started coaching Cathy, I began by working with her to discover and articulate her personal vision, and then coached her to link her personal vision to the organizational vision. Once she made that connection, it all came together. Used in conjunction, personal and organizational vision gave her a solid foundation. She gained both confidence and a greater feeling of control over both her personal and organizational lives. Being laser-focused on her vision, and guided by her values, naturally motivated her to fulfill her purpose. She was able to be a better role model for her team and a better leader for her organization.

Wellness and vision, without leadership

Finally, imagine an executive who excels in wellness and vision, without leadership. These executives achieve great strides in their self-care by taking time for their health, nutrition, fitness, and positive social relationships. They have great dreams, but the dreams never materialize because they do not demonstrate sound leadership.

Jack is an executive many admire. He runs marathons, volunteers as a coach for a local soccer team, and has a solid grasp of the direction his organization needs to go. But his CEO and the people who work for him are frustrated. He was unable to influence or inspire others to follow a specific direction that supports their own interests, as well as that of the organization. There is no solid, strategic plan of action; the "tomorrow" desired from a leadership perspective never becomes "today." Although Jack could be described as both healthy and visionary, he had only developed average leadership abilities, and yet had so much untapped leadership potential. While he had some leadership success, he was not keeping abreast of more current strategies for fostering a better learning environment for the changing employee demographics in his large division.

When I started coaching Jack, I worked with him on the six key leadership competencies that I will discuss later. Within a short period of time, he developed a high level of self-awareness and understood much better how his behaviour impacted others. Working at developing the six leadership competencies turned his performance around. He was able to influence and inspire his staff in a whole new way, providing a much better learning environment for his whole team.

In summary, vision, leadership, and wellness are all pieces of a whole. Separated or off balance, they will never lead to extraordinary success for the corporate executive. But those executives who align all three can lead an unbelievable life.

HOW TO USE THIS BOOK

In my work as an executive coach, you can imagine that one of the most valued commodities I can offer my clients is saving them time. Their focus needs to be accelerating their performance in the organization, as well as achieving a better balance in their personal life. I understand the challenge of information overload and how critical it is to condense what is most important for success. As a result, my objective is to take the most important insights for your success in the twenty-first century and bring it all together for you in one book. Corporate executives need a book that is easy to read, practical, and easy to use; a book that provides them with quick and easy access to the key areas they need to keep them on track for their desired outcomes. I believe that the few hours that you spend reading this book will bring a solid return on investment in terms of what you need to do to move towards your more focused and improved-quality life.

The theme of this book is the importance of aligning vision, leadership, and wellness to achieve extraordinary success. This book aims to inspire you and influence you to maximize your performance while achieving a better balance in life. If you are looking for a book that demonstrates step-by-step instruction and information on the "how-tos" of developing your personal and organizational vision, leadership skills, or wellness, this is not the book for you. That is a whole book in itself.

Certainly, this book is loaded with real life stories, practical examples, and helpful tools. However, this is not a how-to book that covers the three areas in exhaustive detail. This book is about the fundamental importance of *integrating* vision, leadership, and wellness because it is the integration of all three areas that provides the glue for the long-term benefit of the corporate executive. With this investment in sustaining high performance, it's also highly cost effective for organizations.

The book is divided into three broad sections. The first section, with chapters on personal and organizational vision, lays the foundation. Personal vision is your anchor; it's what keeps you on track for what matters to you most. We look at the connection of personal vision to our deepest values, and see how vision helps us stay focused, ignited, and engaged every day with a natural motivation to achieve our objectives. Corporate executives don't work alone, but in organizations and teams, and our personal vision needs to be an excellent match with the organizational vision. The organizational vision chapter highlights the importance of modelling organizational vision and values in behaviour, and supporting a solid leadership culture. I also introduce how critical it is, especially in today's marketplace, to include the values of wellness and work/life balance in organizational vision.

The second section is focused on personal and organizational leadership. The starting point for exceptional personal leadership is self-awareness. To be highly successful, it is absolutely critical for today's leaders to have a high level of integrity, trust, self-awareness, and understanding of how their behaviour impacts others. The personal leadership chapter highlights six key leadership competencies that exceptional leaders must continually develop and practise. These are: strategic thinking; communication, especially active listening; emotional intelligence; negotiating and conflict management; managing energy and time; and mastering lifestyle management and overall wellness. The chapter on organizational leadership provides insights to help you demonstrate your high-caliber personal leadership in the context of your organization. This chapter focuses on strategic-business planning and succession planning as the two critical pillars of organizational leadership, and the necessary architecture for extraordinary organizational success.

The third section is the longest of the book, with two chapters on personal wellness and one chapter on organizational wellness. Wellness and lifestyle management has been an important part of my coaching practice for more than a decade, though it has been so often neglected in business cultures. The personal wellness chapters cover a number of highly integrated topics under the broad umbrellas of physical health management and lifestyle management. Using my experience working with hundreds of corporate executives, as well as consultation with a multitude of health practitioners and many books, I have condensed the insights that are of greatest use to corporate executives and high potential leaders. I know from my coaching experience that these insights on topics such as fitness, nutrition, work/life balance, happiness, and finances can make a huge difference to the personal life, professional performance, and organizational success of a corporate executive.

The conclusion emphasizes the power of aligning vision, leadership, and wellness, and provides some general self-assessment tools for you to begin to evaluate your areas of strength, and identify areas you need to further develop.

LIVE YOUR BEST LIFE NOW

The good news is that I can assure you that the executives in corporate America who have mastered vision, leadership, and wellness are living their best lives now. They are living a quality professional life with a matching quality personal life. It is simpler than you think. Information and knowledge are power. With the understanding and ability to integrate all three areas, it is doable! I know because over the last 20 years of coaching hundreds of clients — from high potential managers to directors to vice-presidents and CEOs — they've mastered it. They are reaping the benefits of their hard work and enjoying a superb quality of life.

Life has become much simpler, yet gratifying for them. They now have an anchor to refer back to when making the short- and long-term key decisions that impact their life. They are more resilient. They are accomplishing much more in life while expending much less energy. You can achieve this too. I invite you to read and learn about the power of *All Together Now*.

PART ONE

Vision

CHAPTER ONE

Personal Vision

FINDING YOUR ANCHOR

Years ago, I sailed from Owen Sound into Georgian Bay in Canada's beautiful North. I travelled with friends on their wooden 37-foot Alberg boat called *Moonfleet*. We arrived in Lion's Head in the late afternoon and anchored in the bay. During the night, a storm blew in and mercilessly rocked the boat. Winds and currents knocked us back and forth. As the storm raged, we listened to the weather forecast and made decisions on how far we would venture for the rest of the weekend. In the morning, calm had returned and we prepared to set sail again. When the sun rose, we saw that we had moved about 30 feet from where we had initially stopped. Even though the boat rocked all night with strong winds, by having the anchor, we were in control enough to continue our journey the next day. We were able to stay on course.

No seasoned sailing navigator would ever consider staying in open water overnight without an anchor. It would be far too dangerous. So, also, would an executive be foolhardy to consider being at the helm of a major corporation or division without an anchor.

Personal vision is your anchor.

When you've developed your personal vision and can articulate it easily, it becomes the anchor that keeps you on track for what matters most. And, when challenges arise, your anchor helps you to keep on course and meet both your personal and organizational needs. You can venture a short distance from your passion and purpose; however, your personal vision is the anchor you can always refer to and keep your life on track. Not only that, when your personal vision is linked with your organizational vision, it naturally further ignites your purpose and passion, and leads to a more gratifying and meaningful life.

This chapter explores why personal vision is so important to maximize performance and achieve a better balance of wellness in life. We will look at the power of self-awareness, and the connection of personal vision to our deepest values. We will learn how vision can help us stay motivated and focused, ignited and engaged every day with a natural motivation to achieve our objectives. And we will see how having a clearly defined personal vision is fundamental to achieving extraordinary success in personal and professional life.

Understanding the importance of personal vision

When I meet corporate executives who want to maximize their performance while achieving a better balance of wellness in their lives, I start with what will become most foundational for them: their personal vision for their life.

The biggest obstacle to getting what you want in life is not knowing exactly *what* you want. Defining your personal vision means figuring out and articulating what gives you purpose and passion in your life. When coaching my executive clients, I often begin the process of defining personal vision with the question, "Why do you get up in the morning?" Living out your personal vision is like igniting an ever-active volcano. It is what fulfills you and propels you in the direction you want to go. A strong personal and organizational vision has huge impact. Some say the flap of a butterfly's wings in Tibet can be felt in the swirl of a thunderstorm over the great lakes in Canada. So also, a vision, whether small or large, can have a ripple effect, and extend its impact far beyond its initial circles. Vision is a journey not a destination, and we never arrive at the finish line. If we do achieve or surpass our desired vision, it tells us we didn't set our standards high enough for our potential. Or, that we need a new vision that further stretches our growth.

Why is having a personal vision so important? Statistics indicate that only about 20 percent of people are working in positions where they are totally fulfilled, positions where they are living out their purpose in life and are energized by making the most of their natural skill set. In other words, these 20 percent of people love their work. They are ignited. They are naturally engaged. But what about the other 80 percent? Which group do you fit in?

Individuals who take the time to work with a seasoned coach to find their anchor — their fundamental personal vision for themselves — have laid the foundation for their success. It's like finding your DNA. Personal vision is a special and unique combination of desire and talent that is exclusive only to you. Harold Kushner's book *How Good do We Have to Be?: A New Understanding of Guilt and Forgiveness* says: "Every human being's life is a story, a unique story that nobody ever lived before and no one will ever live again."[1] What will that story be for you? How do you leave the world a better place? How do you make your unique impact? How gratifying and meaningful it is when we know our purpose and passion in life, what we want our unique story to be. Knowing your personal vision is a natural motivator.

I am humbled to have the privilege and honour to coach top executives and take them to levels beyond their dreams — they work at the process just as hard as I do. Why are the corporate executives I coach so incredibly successful? And why do they keep sustaining their high performance? It all goes back to the discovery of their passion and purpose: their personal vision, their anchor.

ACCELERATING PERSONAL AND ORGANIZATIONAL PERFORMANCE AND SUCCESS

To be highly successful in the twenty-first century, there are two things I know for certain. First, corporate executives need to have a high level of self-awareness. And second, they need to understand how their behaviour impacts others. Executives who are more mindful and attuned to their colleagues and staff are often also more naturally attuned to their own values.

What better way to take your personal and professional life to a whole new level than to capitalize on your self-awareness and integrate it into a unique personal vision that is exclusive and distinct only to you?

Boards of directors and CEOs of progressive organizations always prefer to hire corporate executives who have a solid personal vision and know their passion and purpose in life. With this foundation clearly set, a mountain of clutter is out of the way, for both the individual and the organization. When you know with clarity what you need for contentment in your own life, you naturally focus on linking and extending that passion, purpose, and personal vision to accelerate organizational performance.

Even gifted, skilled, and smart executives can be wooed by enticing financial opportunities, only to learn down the road that this lucrative opportunity has reduced their confidence and made them feel even more insecure. Why? Because they have not been true to their authentic self. Somehow it doesn't feel right; and when things don't feel right, it means that particular job opportunity is not linked to your personal passion, purpose, and vision. If the foundational work of discovering a personal vision is not done prior to jumping into a lucrative opportunity, the rewards that come from that opportunity will often be temporary. Eventually, the stress and demands of that opportunity will surpass the gratification or meaningfulness.

With changing demographics, the growth of emerging markets, and intensifying globalization, finding and retaining top corporate executives will be an enduring challenge for many organizations, regardless of their specific industry. The tougher the problems are to solve, the more vital it is to hire those who can lead and direct an organization through rough times. It is more important than ever for corporations to hire executives who are grounded in their personal vision, and furthermore, can understand how their personal vision links to the organizational vision. Solving problems, creating solutions, and setting successful directions always flow better from a foundation of clarity in your own personal vision.

The rewards of a clear personal vision extend beyond the individual to the organization and its shareholders. An engaged workforce, led by corporate executives — chief executive officers, vice-presidents, and chief financial officers — who are on purpose and focused, can sustain top performance for the organization and be great role models to retain other top talent in the organization.

SETTING THE FOUNDATION WITH A SEASONED EXECUTIVE COACH

Over the years, I have met a number of executives who seemed adamant that they could find their purpose, passion, and personal vision without a seasoned trainer, facilitator, or executive coach.

A few years ago, I met three executives who were clearly struggling to find their personal visions. However, they truly believed that by reading enough books, they would gather enough information for their personal vision to emerge for them with an exclamation of, "Eureka — I have it!"

When I connected with them again recently at a business network event, the feedback from all three was very similar. They excitedly shared with me that they had finally found their vision and passion — or so they thought! When I asked them to share their personal vision with me, it wasn't instant and easy. They could not clearly articulate what it was.

The process of developing, defining, and articulating your personal vision is not easy. It is hard to be objective about yourself. And it's difficult to get laser-focused on what matters most for your life. That's why some of the best learning comes from focused interaction with an expert facilitator, a third party. To get to your best answers, you need to be asked the right questions.

Time is an irreplaceable commodity for most high performing executives. Yet, these three executives had read book after book, reflected, recollected, and gathered information over a period of months and years in an effort to stumble upon their personal vision.

What held them back from negotiating funding for an executive coaching program? Had they used a seasoned executive coach who has a proven track record and is highly trained in facilitating individual and organizational visions, they could have achieved in several coaching sessions what they achieved in two years. In other words, they could have quickly found their purpose, passion, and personal vision, and be living a better quality and more focused life, already having reduced their stress. How valuable is your time? Why not deal with the issues, move forward, and save years of unfocused searching?

John is a senior corporate executive I have known for a number of years. He is exceptionally intelligent, highly skilled in brand management, and had been promoted to president of a division of a Fortune 500 organization. Recently, John shared with me that he had just completed an eight-month experience with his own executive coach.

In the course of our conversation, I asked him if he'd ever like to move from his divisional position to become the president of the entire corporation if given the opportunity. He told me he would not be interested and — more significantly — that he sometimes found his current role boring, particularly performing the same repetitive tasks of analysis over and over, like preparing for board meetings. On the other hand, his position provided an excellent compensation package for him and his family to live the lifestyle they desired.

I asked him what he would do if, for some reason, his current position no longer existed or that the organization was sold. What would have to happen for him in order for him to be in a job that was meaningful for him? I was dumbfounded when he responded, "I have no idea what I'd like to do next."

John's expensive eight-month executive-coaching experience had helped him enhance his leadership skills to accelerate some areas of his performance, and yet, it had not brought him more meaning or satisfaction in his overall life. What was the most important missing piece? The coach didn't facilitate the fundamental process for establishing a solid foundation for the client to build on: John's personal vision. Too often, this is what happens in executive coaching for corporate executives. As a result, neither the executive nor the organization truly reap the benefit of the dollars spent. The reality is that clarifying personal vision provides the greatest return on investment for the individual and the organization. Personal vision is foundational: it is what everything else is built on.

THE POWER OF PURPOSE AND FOCUSING ON THE "WHY"

Think of colleagues, family, or friends who are always busy, busy, busy. Often they wonder why progress isn't happening in some very important areas of their life. If they are not focused, it's no wonder they are frustrated with their lives.

Are you focused on your vision and objectives? Many people are so caught up in "the doing" that they have lost sight of the bigger picture of what they want their personal and professional life to be about. Personal vision is fundamental to the broader purpose of your life; it is the "why" behind what you do. Like the roots of a tree, it is the place from which your personal objectives grow. The activities and tasks of your everyday life are what bring those objectives to life.

In his book *If How-To's Were Enough, We'd All Be Skinny, Rich, and Happy*, Brian Klemmer proposes that about 75 percent of people are activity-oriented. In other words, they do what needs to be done to survive. Their reaction to life might be defined as being in *survival mode*. About 20 percent of people are goal-oriented. They know *what* they want to do; they have objectives, and they often accomplish them. They might be defined as being in *achievement mode*. And finally, only about 5 percent of people are vision-oriented: they know the *why*. Klemmer says that these are the people who can change the world. He writes, "They focus on their vision and every goal they set in some way points them toward their vision. Every action they take moves them toward a goal that puts them one step closer to the fulfillment of their vision."[2] In a nutshell, Klemmer is telling us that goals and objectives or activities without a vision won't work. In other words, "No matter how much energy and enthusiasm we have, much time is wasted without focusing your actions on an overall purpose that connects to the heart. In a nutshell, your efforts need to be focused on your purpose — and your vision should be the 'why' behind all you do in life."[3]

Beginning with a vision allows you to maximize all of your efforts to achieve your desired outcomes. When you align yourself with a purpose greater than yourself, and make sure your objectives are consistent with your vision, you are able to "release the power of focused effort", as Stephen Covey calls it. Covey's book, *The 7 Habits of Highly Effective People*, calls this mode "beginning with the end in mind." He writes, "Instead of fatigue, vision-oriented people experience fulfillment. Instead of disillusionment, they become inspired. Instead of conflict and compromise, they demonstrate integrity. Instead of living the status quo, these people change the world."[4] You can, too.

I often meet corporate executives who mistake their "job" for their "purpose" in life. Earlier in my career, I worked for an international career transition firm where I coached and counselled many Fortune 500 and Fortune 1,000 senior management individuals who were fired from their positions. Some of these corporate executives who had worked for the same firm most of their life simply could not separate their own identity from the identity of their role in the organization.

In her book, *Real Moments*, Barbara De Angelis writes:

> When you mistake your job for your purpose by taking it too seriously, you can get really messed up. You will work too hard, and have a difficult time saying 'no' to anything. And when you start believing that your job is more important than someone else's, or that you're the only one who can do it, or that the work can't survive without your incredible contribution, then it's time for you to retire and grow tomatoes, or at least take an extended vacation in order to get back in tune with what you're really here for. Taking your job too seriously means

that you either don't know you have a purpose
other than your job, or you have temporarily
forgotten what it is.[5]

Srully Blotnick studied 1,500 business school graduates
from 1960 to 1980. He grouped them into two categories.
Category A consisted of graduates who said they wanted to
make money first so that they could then do what they really
wanted to do later in life, after they had taken care of their
financial concerns. Category B consisted of graduates who said
they wanted to pursue their true interests first, feeling confident
that the money would eventually follow. Of the 1,500 graduates
in the survey, 83 percent (1,245 graduates) were in Category
A and 17 percent (255 graduates) were in Category B. After
20 years, there were 101 millionaires in the total group. One
millionaire came from Category A and 100 of the millionaires
came from Category B. As a result, Blotnick concluded, "The
overwhelming majority of people who have become wealthy
have become so thanks to work they found profoundly
absorbing.... Their 'luck' arose from the ... dedication they
gave to an area they enjoyed."[6]

What really matters to you in your life? What unique
mark will you leave on this planet? It won't matter how big
or small that legacy is; it only matters that you leave one. You
can contribute something unique to this world that no one
else can, because no one else has your combination of skills
and characteristics.

Being firmly connected to purpose, passion, and personal
vision is fundamental for success. Time passes so quickly. Life
is not a rehearsal, it's the real deal. Oliver Wendell Holmes
said, "Most of us go to our graves with our music still inside
us." Clarifying and articulating your personal vision is part of
writing the symphony of your completely unique life.

FINDING YOUR PASSION

"Dancing for me is my oxygen," Dwana Smallwood, an Alvin Ailey Dancer, said. "You have to find something that allows you to live, breathe, no matter what's going on in your life. You have to have something to go to. If it's running track, if it's writing a book, if it's teaching children, if it's sewing, if it's dancing, you need to find something that allows you to grow, to be challenged to nourish yourself and the people around you."[7]

I have been a ballroom dancer for almost 15 years. For me, it's the world's best therapy. When I hear the music and I'm in the flow of dancing a beautiful Viennese waltz, a serious tango, a fast cha cha, or even a rumba, my mind is in a total state of peace. It is difficult to articulate, but it is an awesome feeling! Ballroom dance lets me naturally put my heart and soul into what I'm doing. The flow of performance is so fluent and meaningful that in some ways the actions are effortless, and yet so rewarding and deeply fulfilling. Others around me often comment that this passion is contagious as they become more enthusiastic and excited to learn more about their own passions.

In his national bestseller *Flow: The Psychology of Optimal Experience*, Mihaly Csikszentmihalyi talks about optimal experience and the personal traits that help people achieve that flow more easily. Csikszentmihalyi says that the happy state of flow "arises most often in work that stretches a person without defeating him; work that provides 'clear goals,' 'unambiguous feedback' and a 'sense of control.'"[8]

Finding our passion is not only important for us personally, it's important for leaders and executives of organizations who manage and inspire others. The people who are connected to their passions in their work life, and whose leaders understand those passions, are the people that stay in organizations and contribute their best work with energy, enthusiasm, and skill. Dr. Beverly Kaye, co-author of *Love 'Em or Lose 'Em: Getting Good People to Stay*, said in a recent interview, "Managers need to communicate — formally, informally, but on a regular basis — and find out how employees' passions can contribute to the company. Ask questions like 'What about your job makes you jump out of bed in the morning? What makes you press the snooze button?' If you listen carefully, you'll hear passion. When the thrill is gone, so are they."[9]

When I worked in an international career transition firm in my earlier years, I used to tell corporate executives that in making a transition to a new job, they should find a job that utilizes many of the skills they love to use but which they feel guilty getting paid for. That's the real test of knowing you've found your passion. "I love what I do! And I even get paid for doing it!"

When you truly find your passion, you are living authentically. You can't help but naturally, enthusiastically, and effortlessly let the world know what you are excited about. Your facial expressions, excitement, and positive attitude tell your story. You are happy doing what you love to do, and it's natural to want to share that with others. As the saying goes, "True success comes with being at peace with yourself." Some people are old at 30, and some people are young at 80. How is this? Are you living the life you want to live? Are you living your passion? Do you realize that we all have a choice to do that in life? And when you make your choice, do you have the courage and tenacity to stick with it — to be committed — especially when you are challenged and the going gets tough? Or are you willing to change your choice?

CONNECTING TO OUR DEEPEST VALUES

Your beliefs become your thoughts. Your thoughts become your words. Your words become your actions. Your actions become your habits. Your habits become your values. Your values become your Destiny.

— Mahatma Gandhi

The corporate executives I coach have a strong desire to maximize their performance. But sometimes, they have a difficult time expressing why getting to this objective is so difficult for them. They feel like something is not right, but they don't exactly know what it is. Not being able to put their finger on it can cause anxiety or tension.

In my experience, many corporate executives and high-potential leaders are under stress because they are not honouring their key values. They may not initially recognize this as a reality, or even a problem. But if the disconnection from key values is not addressed, little by little this unease will erode their confidence, and begin to increase their mental and physical stress. Often, they are working around others whose values are also at odd with theirs. When that happens, chronic stress is the result.

Our personal vision must be solidly linked to the core elements that give the greatest meaning to life — our values. Our values show up in every realm. On a physical level, for example, our values might include health, comfort, money, or a particular standard of living. On an emotional level, our values related to emotions might include sincerity, honesty, accomplishment, freedom, or belonging. On an intellectual level, our values might include learning, performing, problem solving, creating, or teaching. We may be able to answer the purpose question, "Why do I get up in the morning?" But to truly articulate your vision, purpose must be combined with values. L. Lionel Kendrick says, "Values are the foundation of our character and of our confidence. A person who does not know what he stands for or what he should stand for will never enjoy true happiness and success."[10]

It is surprisingly easy to get unintentionally disconnected from your values over years of working in organizations, or simply living a busy life. As John Blumberg wrote in his recent book *Good to the Core*, "We don't go running away from our values. We go drifting away, and one day wake up in a place we were never meant to be, drifting in a direction we would never have chosen."[11] When this happens, it is often helpful to look back at your childhood dreams. As children, many of us were creative, daring, and bold about what we wanted to accomplish in life. Then, over the years of high school, university, and discussions with parents and career counsellors, we learned more about what we *should* want to do or be. Looking back, though, what did you truly love to do? What were the skills you loved most? What did you fantasize about doing for life? The answers about your life's purpose are hidden within yourself. You need only to be asked the right questions by a skilled coach or facilitator.

Morris Massey, an originator of intergenerational values and beliefs studies, believed that your values and beliefs are locked in by the time you are about 12 years old. What were those seeds of wisdom that inspired you when you were a kid, the ones you slowly let go of as you grew up, and as you allowed others in your life to impact or change your true values? Little by little, many of us have moved away from that early inspirational thinking. Taking time to play with these early memories can often be helpful because they are solidly linked to the values that relate to our childhood dreams. We need to reconnect to the inherent values that have always been in the core of us. Some of our values change and evolve over the years for good reason. However, some of the change does not serve us well. Rather, it leads us away from our true authentic values, the ones that make us feel comfortable in our own skin.

I firmly believe that we are our values. So often, corporate executives who have been in a career for many years gradually begin to say, "I'm not so sure what's changed over the last years, however, something doesn't feel right for me." They feel that they are beginning to lose the magic in sustaining their performances at work, or are dissatisfied with their personal lives. In my 25 years of experience coaching executives, I have learned that, more often than not, the underlying reason for these feelings of insecurity or unease relate directly back to personal vision and values. Corporate executives that don't put their anchor down lose their focus. As a result, how can they be resilient and bounce back when challenges arise, or when the relentless busyness of their lives has worn them down? If they had their anchor of personal vision, they would only drift so far, and then they would get back on track.

FUNDAMENTAL VALUES FOR SUCCESS

To be highly successful in today's business world and to effectively manage this generation of employees, there are three important values that are fundamental to every corporate executive in their personal and professional life: trust, integrity, and humility.

We know that a corporate executive cannot "produce" trust, integrity, or humility. It's not something we manufacture. These values need to be demonstrated consistently in behaviours. And, like a pebble thrown into a pond, these behaviours ripple out to directly and indirectly impact all levels of staff and the culture of the organization.

One of the things I assess when I first meet a coaching client is to learn if the values of the executive and the organization truly include trust, integrity, and humility, or if it is just lip service. Even if executives are arrogant, are they willing to work with a coach on changes required to meet the values of the organization for succession planning and other purposes? If the commitment is not there from the beginning, I turn the assignment away; it will not be cost effective for the organization and will not provide a return on investment. To accept coaching contracts with organizations that lack trust, integrity, and humility would be a waste of time, resources and energy. These values are absolutely fundamental to achieving extraordinary high levels of effectiveness.

Building trust by living with integrity

Integrity is consistently being true to who you are. Plato had it right when he said, "Know thyself." Living with integrity affects how you feel about yourself. When you feel good about yourself, your actions and decisions, it naturally enhances your self-esteem. Integrity is all about "to thine own self be true." This naturally helps create greater positive energy and trust for you as a leader. Integrity is the key to living an authentic life, both personally and professionally. Most highly successful executives clearly articulate their values and demonstrate them consistently. This naturally enhances their relationship with their colleagues and staff.

In her book *Real Moments*, Barbara De Angelis writes, "When you compromise your dreams and your values for someone else's, you give your power away. The more you live as who you truly are, the more peace you will invite in your life. Living with integrity means: not settling for less than what you know you deserve in your relationships; asking for what you want and need from others; speaking your truth, even though it might create conflict or tension; behaving in ways that are in harmony with your personal values; and making choices based on what you believe, and not what others believe."[12]

Regrettably, many people live their life without being authentic, without honouring their own integrity. They let life move along and rarely say what they feel, or act on what they know to be true. It often takes a tragic event — a serious illness, death, family breakdown — to motivate them to reprioritize what is important to them and get back to living their values.

Where are you not telling the truth in your life? Are you aware how costly not dealing with this can be to your future? What standards do you commit yourself to in your personal and professional life? This can be as simple as keeping your promises or commitments to others.

Too many corporate executives have tied up their self-worth with what they do, rather than who they are. This is why executives so quickly lose their confidence when their organization is suddenly downsized, or they lose their job. When they no longer have their position or title, it is a major challenge for their ego. Somehow they have allowed their title to define who they are.

Highly successful and fulfilled executives are defined by authenticity, not title, possessions, or net worth. Their personal gratification and happiness is sustained because it comes from within, not from external forces. There's absolutely nothing wrong with having a high net worth, lots of possessions, or a great title. The key factor is simply that if the high net worth, possessions, or title are your sole identity, you are creating a short time high that will be very unhealthy in the long term. Some executives are living in multimillion-dollar mansions with all the bells and whistles and their own private golf courses. And yet, they can easily fall into the pit of unhappiness and loneliness. Only when they learn that their worth is who they are authentically, not what they do or own, can they align their vision, leadership, and wellness to live the true life of their dreams.

This generation of young adults are more educated and passionate about authenticity than ever before. They are concerned about green living, organic ingredients, high-tech services and gadgets, and more. They are more demanding, and want clarity around the fairness and honesty of pricing. In the wake of corporate financial scandals, this generation is quickly learning that there are corporate executives and organizations that are highly committed to trust, integrity, and honesty, and others that are not. With Twitter and Facebook, and the speed of the Internet, information is travelling faster than ever before. As a result, many of today's organizations are investing in improving their board governance to ensure more transparency for employees and shareholders, not only to make it more inviting for top-talent corporate executives to join their firm, but also to demonstrate this trust, honesty, and integrity to the shareholders of the organization. More than ever before, being authentic with a high level of integrity is fundamental to any long term personal and professional success.

Living with humility

If you had a scale where number one was "arrogant" and number 10 was "humble," where would you plot yourself on the scale?

Humility is not a value that is typically trumpeted in the corporate world. Yet, it has incredible power and importance. When corporate executives are humble, they are much more approachable. This gives them an incredible opportunity to learn more about themselves, as well as their personal and organizational leadership. Feedback from their colleagues and staff can enhance their overall life and performance, and cultivate that self-awareness and an understanding of how their behaviour impacts others — a critical skill for successful executives.

Humility and arrogance are closely related to security and insecurity. Through my coaching process, I am often honoured to have CEOs and corporate executives share some of their deepest insecurities about their role as a leader. My experience is that it is often the most arrogant executives who are the most insecure inside. Arrogance is often a mask for fear. By contrast, the executives I have worked with who are more humble, are usually much more confident and secure. When I first started my coaching practice, I found it interesting that high performers who were already exceptional at their craft were the ones who wanted to use my services. They wanted to take themselves to a whole new level. For the most part, these types of executives were also committed to humility as one of their values. They didn't need to be arrogant to achieve outstanding standards of excellence. In fact, they knew it worked against them and their personal and organizational success. Many of the highly successful and happy corporate executives I know learn early that it is always better to have colleagues, friends, or clients remind the world of their achievements, rather than praise themselves.

Intuitive employees can pick up very quickly if a leader is arrogant and it is a real "turn off" to them. I can almost guarantee — especially with the new generation of employees today — you will not get sustained maximum performance from staff if you demonstrate arrogance in any way. However, demonstrating humility naturally creates a desire for staff to be more involved, more productive, and more motivated to give their best skills and abilities to their role, to you as their boss, and to significantly contribute to the overall objectives of the organization.

OPENING THE FUTURE OF OUR DREAMS

Purpose, passion, and vision are all grounded in our values; they are inextricably linked. Jim Clemmer says our lives, teams, and organizations are shaped by three vital questions: Where am I going? (my vision or picture of my preferred future); What do I believe in? (my principles or values); Why do I exist? (my purpose or mission). "These questions are at the center of our lives," Clemmer writes. "They are central to our choices, authenticity, passion and commitment, spirit and meaning, growth and development, and ability to energize and mobilize others. Visions are values projected into the future. Both flow from purpose. Vision, values, and purpose are interconnected and inseparable. Sometimes they operate like a combination lock. Each twist and turn of the dial doesn't appear to do much, but when they are all lined up, the future we dream of clicks open."[13]

Achieving clarity around passion, purpose, values, and vision is incredibly powerful. Ask yourself, "If I had all the money in the world, what would I do?" If you would answer, "I'd do exactly what I'm doing," you know that you are living right at the centre of your personal vision. So often, we are pressured to do what everyone else thinks we should be doing, instead of what we ourselves value and are passionate about. When you are doing what you love in life, you will be at peace within yourself, and much more likely to be at peace with others — including your family, friends, organization, and community.

Cheryl Richardson says, "At the time you were born you were given an amazing gift — a gift that most of us forget about as we grow older. It's the power to design your own unique life. You are an artist. The canvas is your life. From this moment on, take ownership of this gift and use it wisely. If you do, your life will become an extraordinary work of art."[14]

What is your personal vision? Is it alive in your life? Are you living it daily? What needs to happen for you in this life that would allow you to "live on purpose"? Are you making your life an extraordinary work of art? Remember: keep your personal vision simple — less is more. Like an arrow lodged in the bull's eye of an archery target, the more simple your personal vision is, the more simple it is to stay laser-focused and to measure your progress.

CHAPTER TWO

Organizational Vision

OPENING THE DRAWER

Organizational vision is the *raison d'être* or purpose of the organization. It is a general statement about why the organization exists and what the organization wants to become in the *future*. The vision statement needs to be future-oriented, because it indicates where the organization is headed, its direction, and desired contributions to the business world and society. Organizational vision should be accompanied by a set of core values that determine how an organization operates its business.

Before embarking on other strategic business plans, it is critical to develop the organizational vision and set of core values first. Only then can a highly effective mission be defined. Why? The mission is a statement about the purpose of the organization in the *present*. The mission statement needs to be present-oriented because it indicates what the organization needs to be working on now in order to move in the direction of the future vision. A mission statement is more concrete and specific than a vision statement. In response to internal and external influences, mission statements may evolve over an organization's life cycle. However, despite any changes to an organization's mission, the mission statement must always be built on the foundation of the vision statement and set of core values.

Organizational vision and values are not created lightly. Organizational leaders pour a lot of work into creating them, and are highly committed to living them out in practice. Articulating and disseminating this vision and its related behaviours throughout the organization, including the executive's team, helps clarify decision making, and promotes effectiveness and efficiency. Keeping the organizational vision front and centre allows for the appropriate focus in key operational areas, such as customer satisfaction, employee satisfaction, shareholder satisfaction, and product/service delivery excellence. Only decisions that support the values reflected in the organizational vision are allowed to be executed. In the same way, new alternatives are pursued only if they are aligned with the organizations vision and values.

Sounds easy right?

The concept of organizational vision is as old as the hills. Yet, my experience is that executives often develop, design, and create an organizational vision with a set of core values, and then step off that platform and forget about it as they focus on their strategic business plans. Not only that, as the days and weeks march forward, they seldom refer to either. The executive team often experiences a tremendous high after participating in creating an exceptional vision, mission, set of core values, and outstanding business plan, but they fail to refer back to the vision to keep it alive. The vision and strategic business plan are filed away in a neat report, the task closed and completed.

Over the years, I have facilitated hundreds of sessions for organizations to create their organizational visions and develop their strategic business plans. Achieving extraordinary success doesn't happen from a closed file folder in a drawer. It happens from the integration of vision, leadership, and wellness on both the personal and organizational level — The All Together Now Advantage. This chapter dives more deeply into the importance of organizational vision. Using research, real-life stories, and experience, I begin with the importance of living out organizational vision and values in practice. With high potential leaders and executives in mind, the chapter then talks about the importance of modelling organizational vision and values in behaviour, and supporting a solid leadership culture. I explain how critical it is, especially in today's marketplace, to include the values of wellness and work/life balance in organizational vision. Finally, I get us back to the overall theme of integration, how important it is to align personal and organizational vision, and to integrate not just vision, but leadership and wellness to achieve extraordinary success.

LIVING OUT ORGANIZATIONAL VISION
AND VALUES IN PRACTICE

Vision and values must be linked to behaviours, otherwise they are meaningless. With advance organizational commitment to a vision and set of values, it is easier to deal with staff who do not adhere to these values. For example, some corporate executives have low impulse control (an element of emotional intelligence which can be improved with coaching). When such executives demonstrate negative behaviours, such as bad tempers, being disrespectful to others, or making others feel unnecessarily anxious and cautious, it is unacceptable. In fact, progressive organizations are no longer tolerating this type of behaviour. It is simply not worth it in the long run for the organization. For the most part, these executives have no idea how badly their behaviour can damage others and negatively impact productivity. They may not know it, but they can also indirectly impact profits of the organization: staff on their team won't be as willing to share their creative ideas with executives who are not approachable. If the behaviour does not change over a reasonable period of time, the organization needs to refer to their set of core values and make the appropriate decision. That could mean terminating the executive. Organizations today know that values are key.

Some organizations are successful, well-known, and highly regarded, even in the global marketplace. However, if the organization's written vision and values do not fit with its behaviour and real life practices, its reputation will gradually erode and it will only have short-term success. The vision and values may actually be posted on the office wall, but over time, the organization will become suspect, and will be categorized alongside others that have been judged to lack integrity, authenticity, and trust.

Modelling organizational vision and values in behaviour

For organizations to be highly effective, vision and values must go beyond writing on the wall. What takes organizational vision and values from the written form and turns them into action is leadership. Effective leadership makes organizational vision come alive. That is why it is absolutely critical that an organization's leaders model the organizational vision and values in their own behaviour and within their teams. The walk must match the talk.

A senior management colleague of mine was recently interviewed for a job with a leading-edge organization that markets and sells high-tech devices. From her chair in the reception area, she had a perfect view of the organization's written vision and values statements, which were hung on the wall in an attractive frame. As she waited for her appointment, she read the organizational values of respect, responsiveness, innovation, and so forth. Over the course of the next hour, she made several polite inquiries to the receptionist about how much longer the delay would be for her interview. Eventually, she struck up a conversation with another candidate in the reception area, a recent computer-science graduate who was eagerly awaiting one of the first interviews he had ever had with a corporation. She learned that he had been waiting for almost two hours! Not surprisingly, my friend began to doubt whether the organizational values of respect and responsiveness were more than just writing on a beautifully framed plaque on the wall.

Supporting a solid leadership culture

An essential element of the core vision for any organization in today's marketplace is the development of leaders. It is only by consistently developing leaders that organizations gather their competitive edge. While most products are competitive, the true edge is in the people — the talent and skill set of the organization. The ultimate competitive edge of the organization is the ability to grow and develop leaders faster and better than the competition. This also allows the organization to have momentum for succession planning.

Part of developing leaders is creating a leadership culture. The Four Seasons has an internationally successful global chain of luxury hotels. Isador Sharpe started the chain as a 29-year-old, and is now recognized as one of Canada's most successful businessmen. Sharpe knows that "Money and property will take you only so far. A culture cannot be copied, it cannot be imitated. It has to grow from within over a very long time, based upon the consistent action of senior management. *That* is the barrier to entry for other hotels trying to compete against us. It isn't just having a fine building."[1]

The most progressive organizations have leadership development at the very core of their organizational vision. Not only that, they consistently lead the pack. When economic times are tough and profits are low, some organizations panic, stop training leaders, and lose their best talent. By contrast, organizations that value and invest in leadership development are poised and ready to go with full-fledged leaders when the economy rebounds.

In my experience, I have found that it is very easy for organizations to cancel or delay training and development as a short-term cost-reduction activity. However, the long-term impact on the organization is that when the economy turns around, they do not have the leadership talent to take advantage or leverage the economic recovery. In other words, they can't rebound as fast as the economy does. Leadership is about long-term return on investment; reactive, short-term mechanisms will sabotage long-term organizational effectiveness at the leadership level.

Embracing the value of wellness and work/life balance in organizational vision

Today's marketplace requires a unique set of values for organizational effectiveness and efficiency. To attract and retain top talent, today's organizations need to ensure respect for employees, diversity, work/life balance, and wellness. The new generation of employees says, "I'll work hard for the organization. In return, I want to be paid fairly and to maintain my marketability." This means organizations need to invest in these talented people, and follow through on their promises. Employees are the true strength of an organization, as well as its ultimate competitive edge, and they need to be treated that way.

Effective organizations understand and embrace diversity, in terms of gender, ethnicity, and age, for example. Good leaders appreciate input from people who think differently from the rest of their team. Many of today's employees have global experience and can provide insight from different perspectives.

In my work with high potential leaders and executives, it is not uncommon to hear comments from a senior level executive that go something like this: "This organization is about making profits for the shareholders. It's not about work/life balance, it's not about wellness. That's the responsibility of the employee not us." Far from it! Today's reality is that work and home life are a blur when it comes to wellness and performance. Best practice employers, and organizations that are able to compete at the highest levels, embrace the values of wellness and work/life balance, and include them right at the core of their organizational vision. They provide things like healthy, nutritious cafeterias, fitness facilities, and yoga classes, for example, or they provide subsidies for employees to use these services.

ENSURING PERSONAL VISION AND VALUES ARE ALIGNED WITH THE ORGANIZATIONAL VISION AND VALUES

Just as a personal vision grounds each executive in what really matters in his or her life, so does the organizational vision ground the organization in what really matters for the organization. The organizational vision provides the clarity for each team member to identify how she or he can be more engaged and actively participate in the desired outcomes. The effective executive ensures that the organizational vision is an excellent match with the values reflected in his or her personal vision. When this happens, the executive becomes and stays naturally motivated, ignited, and empowered to take whatever reasonable action to ensure the implementation of the values in the organizational vision. When it doesn't happen, the executive operates in a state of frustration, unfulfillment, and even chronic stress, all of which makes for both low morale and compromised performance.

I learned this the hard way. Early in my career, I worked for an international career-transition organization. Although it provided me with exceptional training, within the first two months I realized that there was a major misfit with my values and the values of this particular organization. Fortunately, I was able to take lemons and make lemonade; I used the experience to dig deeper for insights on the incredible importance of values. Looking back at photos from that time period tells the tale. Though I worked for the organization for less than a year, by the end of that year, I looked five years older than I did many years later. It was a high price to pay. What a great relief it was to leave that organization and join the broadcasting industry, where I quickly regained my youthful appearance and became myself again by working in an environment that was a good fit with my values. The redeeming factor is that I consistently use that personal experience to illustrate the link between values and overall health and quality of life. The simple lesson is that when values do not fit, it plays great havoc on the body. Positive stress supports the growth of positive cells in the body and keeps you healthy. A poorly fitting values system is linked to bad stress which often becomes chronic, producing many negative cells in the body, which make you sick. Your mind and body know inuitively if the fit for values feels good or not. Your job is to listen, and take appropriate action. There is always an organization that will have the right fit and values for you. Knowing yourself and what you need is always the first step.

Unfortunately, many executives have not established their personal vision. Too many people who are graduating with university degrees, or beginning work in the business world, are schooled to focus on their business needs first. However, there is no question that it is much wiser and more effective to focus on personal vision first: that is what sets the foundation. Some people may ask, "Who is responsible for me to develop a personal vision — me or the organization?" I firmly believe that high-potential candidates and corporate executives deserve the services of a coach or facilitator to help them craft that personal vision, which is crucial to sustaining long-term performance for the organization and is best combined with other leadership development. Most progressive firms that are highly committed to their people and profits will support executive coaching or leadership training for their executives. Not only that, over time, high-potential leaders will migrate to those kinds of organizations because they "get it." This becomes a great passionate exchange — outstanding skills and contribution by the high-potential leader or executive, and an organization keeping them marketable in return for their contribution — for the overall purpose of organizational vision and profitability.

Luke De Sadeleer and Joseph Sherren remind us of the power of the connection between personal vision and values, and organizational vision and values. They write, "Values represent your most basic fundamental beliefs. They are the principles that will arouse an emotional reaction, if you perceive them to be threatened. They can also spur on your greatest achievements. If your work incorporates your values, you are likely to find that what you do is meaningful, purposeful and important."[2] Moreover, Anne Greenblatt from Stanford University says, "When your work is aligned with your values, you tap into the 'fire within.' The highest achievements of people and organizations arise when people feel inspired to accomplish something that fits their top values."[3]

Linking personal vision and values with organizational vision and values happens best when executives are active participants in putting the organizational vision together. I often work with organizations that are looking for a CEO or other key senior executive candidate. A common question is, "Is it best to move forward and facilitate an organizational vision and set of core values, or to wait until they have hired the new executive?" My view is that if the executive being hired is so essential to the organization, it is much more practical and cost effective for the organization to wait until that person is hired, and allow them to be a key participant in creating or redeveloping a vision and set of core values for the organization. After all, the new person, with the support of their team, will be a central figure for promoting the vision and making it happen. And the best way to do that is to ensure the organizational vision is also compatible with the personal vision and values of the new executive.

In other situations, an executive starts working with an organization whose vision and values have been handed down in writing over the years by the founders, and it's not possible to change them. In this case, it's even more important for the executive to ensure his personal vision and values are aligned with those of the organization he is joining, and that the organizational vision and values are still relevant and meaningful to the current generation of employees and customers.

INTEGRATING VISION, LEADERSHIP, AND WELLNESS

Organizational and personal vision are incredibly important. But they are only one piece of the puzzle.

Most executives I meet are smart, capable people. Many of them are exceptional in terms of defining vision *or* practicing leadership *or* living a life of wellness. Unfortunately, most executives see vision, leadership, and wellness as separate. As a result, they never get to leverage all three in order to achieve extraordinary success and live the life of their dreams.

I have met only a handful of corporate executives over the two and a half decades of my career who have mastered the integration of all three areas — and they are living the lives of their dreams. In my work with executives, those executives who master this integration become laser-focused on what matters most for them in their life, they develop and stay focused on their personal vision, and ensure their personal vision is linked to their organizational vision. Their objectives and life goals are aligned with key areas of accountability in their organization. Further, by leveraging vision, leadership, and wellness, they give themselves the gift of time. Integrating all three of these elements allows them to perform at a higher level, and achieve so much more in both their personal and professional lives. More than that, they accomplish high levels of performance, while expending less energy. They are stimulated by their positive challenges instead of being kept up at night worrying about things over which they have little control. And they are living meaningful lives where they love getting out of bed in the morning. What a difference to health and performance that makes!

Those who have not mastered this integration of vision, leadership, and wellness are working way too hard to achieve their desired outcomes. Mastering the integration and achieving extraordinary success are possible — if you are willing to do the work. I have met many executives who, as they get older, realize there was so much more in life they wanted to do, experience, and accomplish, but it never happened. Regrettably, as time goes on, many of them are not in good enough physical condition to do those things they wanted to do. Many corporate executives work long hours, burn out, and try to make as much money as they can. Some who have overworked most of their lives get ill, and would give all the money they have to simply live their lives over again in a different way. Don't let this be you. By aligning personal and organizational vision, you are making an important first step.

PART TWO

Leadership

CHAPTER THREE

Personal Leadership

EXCEPTIONAL LEADERSHIP AND SELF-AWARENESS

Exceptional leaders define their personal vision, align it with organizational vision and values, and then inspire people to embrace that vision and make it happen. Along the way, they find ways to allow people to celebrate their own successes. They are also excellent role models, fostering a healthy learning environment in the teams they lead where others can maximize their individual potential and become significant contributors to the organization.

Many books have been written about corporate leadership. My many years of coaching corporate executives tells me that to achieve extraordinary success in both personal and organizational life, the magic is not only in leadership, but in the integration of leadership, vision, and wellness. It is aligning and leveraging all three that leads to high performance, with less energy, and more meaningful rewards.

In order to achieve outstanding success as a leader in today's business world, there is one prerequisite. It is absolutely critical that you have a high level of self-awareness. You need to understand how your behaviour impacts others, including the teams you lead, your clients, and others in your organization. After all, how can executives positively influence others until they understand themselves first?

Robert Galford and Anne Seibold Drapeau, authors of *The Trusted Leader*, summarize it this way:

> If you strip away all but the essentials, being a trusted leader is about knowing yourself. Knowing your strengths, your shortcomings, what gives you pleasure, what annoys the hell out of you. Knowing why you go to work, why you react as you do under pressure, what scares you, and what makes you proud. The true trusted leaders we know all have one thing in common, if nothing else: They know themselves very well...You must first be comfortable in your own skin. And you must also be able to share your understanding of yourself with others, so that their expectations will be in line with your delivery. Above all else, trusted leadership means not faking it.[1]

In a 2010 study of three-hundred top executives in over 40 countries, Robert Rosen and his colleagues from Healthy Companies International identify being genuine as one of the top five characteristics of the best leaders. Knowing yourself, knowing your business, and being forthright about your strengths and weaknesses are some of the most pivotal qualities of exceptional leaders.[2]

When I first begin a coaching program, many of the corporate executives think they already have a high level of self-awareness and understand how their behaviour impacts others. However, the reality is that after they complete a managerial/behaviourial assessment, which scientifically validates their natural inherent characteristics, including what motivates them, they usually discover things about themselves they did not know.

Cultivating exceptional personal leadership means taking the initiative to raise your level of self-awareness. With that knowledge, you will be more effective in leading and influencing others on your team and in the organization. You will have great clarity and understand more about how your behaviour impacts others.

Many of today's newly hired employees have no respect for position power or the importance of hierarchy in the organization. Today's employees follow a leader not because of his or her title, but only if that leader has the ability to provide them with the information and support they need to improve their performance, grow on the job, and stay marketable.

As a corporate executive, are you relying on position power or on your leadership skills to get results? Your ability to align the personal growth objectives of your employees with the organization's vision and strategies will determine whether or not you have committed followers. Or if you are really working alone.

SIX KEY LEADERSHIP COMPETENCIES FOR A COMPETITIVE EDGE

For a competitive edge in today's business world, high-potential leaders and corporate executives need to practice six key leadership competencies. Of course, it's not what you know, it's how you use it. Knowledge is not skill: you can read as many books about golf as you want, but that won't make you a great golfer. The key question is, can you play golf and get excellent results? In the same way, these leadership competencies have to be performed and practised to be mastered. Leadership development is a lifetime process and not a one-time event.

The latest research on what separates star executives from their peers, and what elevates top chief executives and their organizations beyond the competition, indicate that certain skills and attitudes push exceptional leaders over the top. For example, Dr. Justin Menke's recent book *Executive Intelligence: What All Great Leaders Have* summarizes eight years of research on intelligence tests and cognitive skills, as well as interviews with hundreds of senior executives and some of the top CEOs in the world. His research concludes that a particular set of skills and aptitudes are the heart of star executive performance.[3] In my experience, and from all the research evidence, I know that it is not personality or style that predicts performance. *It is behaviour that predicts performance.* That is also why, in my coaching practice, I mainly use scientifically validated tools to evaluate specific skills that can be measured and improved. Ironically, many organizations recruit based on personality or style, only to discover in short order that the person they have hired does not have the inherent skills required for the position.

It has been said that a true hero is an ordinary person who has an extraordinary desire and commitment to achieve their best. The following sections highlight six key leadership-skill areas that exceptional leaders continually develop and practice. Mastering these leadership-skill areas naturally accelerates an executive's ability to achieve extraordinary success in both personal and organizational life.

No executive can be successful without having an effective team around him or her to help bring the organization's vision and mission to life. Leaders are only leaders insofar as they have followers, and followers in the corporate context are first and foremost the executive's team. Though this is not a book about team building, strong leaders express these six key leadership competencies in the context of a team. Each competency, developed and practised well, improves team and organizational effectiveness.

The six key leadership competencies are:

1. Strategic thinking
2. Communication, especially active listening
3. Emotional intelligence (EQ)
4. Negotiating and conflict management
5. Managing energy and time
6. Mastering lifestyle management and overall wellness

1. Strategic Thinking

Successful individuals from all walks of life, whether executives, athletes, scientists, politicians, or entrepreneurs, will be the first to tell you that their continued success is a direct result of the attention they pay to strategic thinking and strategic planning. It allows them to make the best use of their resources in the fastest possible time to achieve their personal and organizational results. The unique strategy that executives choose to bring their objectives alive and engage their team is, of course, the key to their success. Exceptional strategic thinking ensures the best use of the limited available resources to support the strategic business plan and objectives of the organization. Strategic thinkers gather and integrate information from internal and external sources, and use this knowledge as a framework for setting direction and developing strategy in line with corporate objectives.

Strategic thinking is deeply tied to learning how to be a visionary. Personal vision is the anchor that keeps us centred in life, and creates the foundation for our success. We then need to ensure that our personal vision is aligned with our organizational vision. Our strategic plans should then be grounded in that organizational vision and core values. Exceptional leaders are enthusiastic role models for their team and others, moving the organization toward realizing that vision.

To be visionary, we must be able to think strategically. We need to have an image of what we want our organization to look like in two, three, or even five years, and then develop the plans to move the organization towards realizing that image. We need to be able to separate what is important from what is urgent for the organizational bigger picture. Executives who spend the majority of their time on today's issues are acting tactically, and in many cases reactively, robbing themselves and their corporations of the opportunity to influence the future of the organization through solid and focused strategic planning.

Too often, executives don't convey their vision clearly and effectively. Their strategic business plans are in a drawer and are not adhered to because they never "came alive" and weren't solidly linked to the direction of the organization. The executive who has not mastered the skill of strategic thinking tends to spend his time in the day-to-day operation of the organization constantly trouble-shooting and fighting fires. The organization easily becomes more reactive than proactive, and the results achieved on the major objectives are hit and miss.

By contrast, executives know they have an excellent grip on strategic thinking when, using Stephen Covey's language, they "keep the end in mind," and they have the habit of always putting "first things first" before deciding on a course of action. If an executive makes a decision without knowing that it will definitely lead him to achieving his most critical objectives, then he has allowed himself to be distracted. The result will be a waste of the limited resources available, and an unnecessary delay in reaching the objectives.

One of my recent coaching clients was brilliant at developing his strategic thinking skills. How could you tell? He visualized the organization's business, desired outcomes, and activities of his division from a strategic or long-term perspective. When working with his team, he integrated various strategic and divisional plans into an overall corporate direction. He took the time to understand broad trends and technology, and to seriously consider their potential applicability to the organization and his division. He fostered a learning environment, where he involved his staff in researching the areas that related most to their interests for supporting the plan. As an executive, he balanced and linked long-term strategy with short-term tactics. He also ensured that he and his staff thought about the issues from both a global and local perspective. In a nutshell, his strategic thinking created a foundation for him to effectively convey the vision and strategic business plans to the organization and his division by keeping the end in mind.

2. Communication, especially active listening

We often assume that executives have leading-edge communication skills. Certainly, for most executive positions, excellent presentation and writing skills are a fundamental requirement. A multitude of workshops focus on strengthening these areas; an executive coach with expertise in these areas can also integrate them into a customized coaching program.

However, at the executive level, communication is not just about being able to prepare a compelling presentation to the rest of the organization, clients, or media. The most important communication skill for exceptional leadership is not only speaking, but listening. Excellent listening skills give us the edge to better understand others. Excellent listening naturally helps build trust and win the respect of others, while poor listening distorts much of the information shared among leaders, managers, teams, and staff. This lack of communication adds cost to the organization. Psychologist and author Carl Rogers says that "The biggest block to personal communication is man's inability to listen intelligently and skillfully to another person."[4] In corporate culture, Bob Gernon, author of *Body & Soul: Unleashing the Power of Your*

Team, reminds us of the incredible consequences of careless listening, whereas efficient listening actually saves us time, money, and our very human relationships.[5]

Many people don't differentiate between "hearing" and "listening." What's the difference?

"Hearing" is the physical process of receiving sound waves. "Listening" is the mental process that sorts through the information in sound. Listening takes much more energy than hearing since it is an activity that involves our whole selves.

Tony Allesandra says there are five basic reasons we fail to listen well.[6] Firstly, listening takes effort. It's more than just keeping quiet, as it involves concentrating on the other person. Secondly, with computers, TV, radio, books, magazines, and other distractions, there is enormous competition for our attention. With all these incoming stimuli, we have learned to screen out information we deem irrelevant. Unfortunately, we also unintentionally screen out things that are important. Thirdly, we think we already know what someone is going to say. We assume that we have a full understanding right from the start, so we jump in and interrupt. We don't take the time required to hear people out. In my experience, this is a huge trap for executives and high-potential leaders.

The fourth reason we don't listen well has to do with the speed gap — the difference between how fast we talk and how fast we listen. The average person speaks at about 135 to 175 words a minute, but comprehends at 400 to 500 words a minute. For the person who is not listening well, that's plenty of time to jump to conclusions, daydream, plan a reply, or mentally argue with the speaker. At least that's how poor listeners spend the time.

And the fifth reason we don't listen well is because we simply don't know how. To be highly effective, executives need to focus more diligently on listening skills. Yet, I am willing to bet that you have taken courses in effective speaking or presentation skills and none on effective listening.

Exceptional leaders cultivate their skills in "active listening." Active listening is more than listening to the content of the speaker's words. It means paying attention to the tone of voice, gesture, facial expression, and body language of the person speaking to you, as well as taking the time to clarify, paraphrase, and summarize what the other person has said to make sure you truly understand. Active listening is a two-way process.

Active listening is one of the greatest motivators for employees. When an employee's ideas and concerns are truly listened to, they experience respect and trust, which naturally motivates them to perform at their highest level. Successful executives make sure to find out what motivates and de-motivates their staff, because it helps support a motivating leadership culture and highly productive working environment.

Greg Voisen (no relation) of the Voisen Cooperative in San Diego says that instead of active listening, our modern experience is to have "continual partial attention." With continual partial attention, we may be speaking to others, but it never really sinks in.

By contrast, when we actively listen, our attentiveness provides the other person with a gift of respect, and allows us to hear so much more than their actual words. In order to be attentive, we need to clear our minds of other thoughts and use our senses to take in all we can about what the other person is saying. Being highly attentive provides us with insights that can then allow us to adjust our own behaviour to meet the needs of the situation.

When successful leaders listen to others, they make sure they are not being distracted by things around them, including cellphones and BlackBerrys. That shows respect. Even if the other person hesitates, active listeners encourage people to speak, and they get clarification to be sure they understand what the speaker is saying. It is important to withhold judgment about other people's ideas until they have had a chance to finish speaking. Be careful not to anticipate what you think they will be saying: even if the anticipation is unintentional, it is only natural to stop listening attentively. In short, successful leaders with exceptional communication skills are able to concentrate on the message from the other person's perspective versus their own perspective. They listen to what is said, confirm what they have heard, and then respond.

Are you an active listener? If so, you are an exception. Listening is a skill that we must continually develop and practise. When senior management treats the staff on their team with respect and dignity, and demonstrate that through active listening, they will get much more productivity from their employees. For the most part, managers and employees want to belong and be part of helping the organization move forward. Which organization would you prefer to work in, the one where the CEO or senior manager actively listens to the conversation you are having with them? Or the one who is "hearing" you and trying to collect messages on their BlackBerry at the same time?

The most highly successful executives I have coached never multi-task. They do one thing at a time, and they get it right the first time, because they are clearly focused on what needs to happen. They understand that preconceived ideas, personal biases, and stereotyping can easily cause them to get lazy in their active listening skills. They work at staying sharp at their communication and listening skills, because they know how critical they are to their success.

3. Emotional Intelligence (EQ)

In today's competitive marketplace, success demands more than just traditional intelligence or IQ. For high-potential leaders or corporate executives to achieve extraordinary success, they must also master the leadership skill area of emotional intelligence — often called EQ.

Emotional intelligence is the ability to be aware of, make sense of, and make use of our emotional competencies to guide our thinking in action. For the most part, corporate executives with a high EQ tend to demonstrate a high level of executive effectiveness. Certainly, having a high EQ does not necessarily mean that the executive is a better leader. However, when executives can utilize their logical analytical business sense alongside a highly developed emotional intelligence, they are much more likely to achieve extraordinary success. My experience is that executives with a naturally high EQ also adapt more quickly to the challenge of aligning vision, leadership, and wellness. Further, they understand that by hiring emotionally intelligent people, or enhancing their own and their staff's EQ skills, they will also enhance overall decision making, productivity, and results in the organization. If an executive's EQ is low, it is a distinct disadvantage.

The concept of EQ has sparked myriad books and theories. This section will summarize some insights I have gained about the key areas of EQ that most positively — and negatively — impact executive effectiveness. The good news is, emotional-intelligence skills can be identified, developed, and mastered. Daniel Goleman, Richard Boyatzis, and Annie McKee's book *Primal Leadership: Learning to Lead with Emotional Intelligence* note, "Great leaders, the research shows, are made [not born], as they gradually acquire in the course of their lives and careers the competencies that make them so effective. The competencies can be learned, at any point. The challenge of mastering leadership is a skill like any other, such as improving your golf game or learning to play slide guitar. Anyone who has the will and motivation can get better at leading, once he understands the steps."[7]

My executive coaching work has taught me that when executives practise and reinforce the right skills, they accelerate their progress. By excelling in their strengths and continuing to work on any areas of development or weakness, they can soar like an eagle. After all, no one ever totally eliminates their areas of weakness — that would make them perfect, and no one is perfect. On the other hand, by appreciating our weaknesses as gifts, they help us to be more humble and often create great new learning experiences. Practise, practise, and more practise is what helps to improve the EQ competency they are working on.

Dr. Reuven Bar-On is an internationally known expert and pioneer in the field of emotional intelligence. His Emotional Quotient Inventory lists 15 emotional competencies.[8] These personal, emotional, and social skills influence our ability to be successful in our daily tasks or challenges, and to cope with the environmental demands and pressures around us. You can read Dr. Bar-On's competency list below.

INTRAPERSONAL (self-awareness and self-expression):
- Self-Regard (being aware of, understanding and accepting ourselves)
- Emotional Self-Awareness (being aware of and understanding our emotions)
- Assertiveness (expressing our feelings and ourselves nondestructively)
- Independence (being self-reliant and free of emotional dependency on others)
- Self-Actualization (setting and achieving goals to actualize our potential)

INTERPERSONAL (social awareness and interaction):
- Empathy (being aware of and understanding how others feel)
- Social Responsibility (identifying with and feeling part of our social groups)

- Interpersonal Relationship (establishing mutually satisfying relationships)

STRESS MANAGEMENT (emotional management and control):
- Stress Tolerance (effectively and constructively managing our emotions)
- Impulse Control (effectively and constructively controlling our emotions)

ADAPTABILITY (change management):
- Reality Testing (validating our feelings and thinking with external reality)
- Flexibility (coping with and adapting to change in our daily life)
- Problem Solving (generating effective solutions to problems of an interpersonal and intrapersonal nature)

GENERAL MOOD (self-motivation)
- Optimism (having a positive outlook and looking at the brighter side of life)
- Happiness (feeling content with ourselves, others and life in general).

In my experience, most corporate executives are already fairly competent in seven of these competencies: assertiveness, independence, self-actualization, social responsibility, flexibility, problem solving, and optimism. Of course this is not always the case, and there is always room for improvement, progress, and growth. However, in many cases, competence in these seven areas is a key factor behind a high-level executive's past achievements, as well as his or her promotions to the senior level.

However, I have also discovered that it is the other eight emotional competencies that typically require much more development. We can call these "the great eight." These eight emotional competencies are: self-regard, emotional self-awareness, empathy, interpersonal relationship, stress tolerance, impulse control, reality testing, and happiness. These emotional competencies are especially critical when you consider that for executives to be successful, they must operate with the support and energy of their team fully behind them. While all of "the great eight" are important, let me highlight two of them that, if not mastered, will prevent you from achieving extraordinary success.

The first is emotional self-awareness. This is likely the most important emotional intelligence competency of all. Executives with a high level of emotional self-awareness are more likely to tune in to how others are feeling, and to address conflict early. Sometimes in a coaching session, executives will share with me that they do not understand a portion of the 360 Feedback they receive, because they believe they are already practising the appropriate behaviours that participants say they are not demonstrating.

Have you ever taken a golf or tennis lesson from a professional, and been shown that certain areas of your body are not in the correct form to hit a great ball? And all the while, you believed you were already practising the proper form? We cannot observe ourselves objectively while we are actively doing something. The right coach with the right skills can work with high-potential leaders or corporate executives to help them accelerate in certain areas — whether it is one-on-one coaching in sports or leadership. If executives do not understand, develop, or tweak their emotional self-awareness, too many other risks are created in their leadership work that can negatively impact either the executive, the organization, or, more likely, both.

The second of the "great eight" emotional competencies I'd like to highlight as a particular challenge for some executives is impulse control. Dr. Bar-On defines it as "the ability to resist or delay an impulse, drive or temptation to act. It entails a capacity for accepting one's aggressive impulses, being composed, and controlling aggression, hostility, and irresponsible behavior."[9] Instead of being able to weigh issues, assess options, and make considered decisions, executives with poor impulse control may be described as rash, hot-headed, or impatient. As Steven J. Stein and Howard E. Book note in their book *The EQ Edge: Emotional Intelligence and our Success*, "No one suggests that effective impulse control involves stifling or disregarding valuable gut feelings. Instead, it is the capacity to look before you leap, to manage a wide range of volatile emotional states and urges wisely and coolly."[10] It's okay to be passionate about an issue, but it's not okay to have a temper tantrum. Very often, the damage of an executive's outbursts is impossible to retract. Victims of such outbursts may take a long time to heal from their wounds and regain their respect for the executive. Further, the behaviours that are modelled at the top of the organization are the ones that cascade down the levels of the staff as acceptable or unacceptable. Lack of impulse control among senior executives negatively impacts the entire organizational culture.

These eight competencies, which typically require more development in executives, greatly affect overall executive effectiveness and can make the difference in achieving extraordinary success, particularly in today's market place. When an executive lacks development of these eight key EQ competencies, it is like they are trying to run against a strong wind. They try to be strong and forceful, but it is a waste of energy. Without question, to achieve extraordinary success as an executive, these eight emotional competencies must be developed.

I have spent the last 15 years of my career working with executives on integrating vision, leadership, and wellness, including developing these emotional competencies. Developing a customized coaching plan using a variety of tools and approaches, including scientifically validated EQ assessments, past performance reviews, data from 360 Feedback results, etc., is key to progress in this area. My experience is that growth and development in these EQ competencies are not only possible, they are essential. Coaching executives in these areas is challenging and difficult work, both for the coach and the executive. However, the rewards are so great for the candidate, their organization, their team, and often their personal and family relationships, that it is well worth the effort. As an executive coach, it is tremendously gratifying for me to design and develop a customized coaching program that will help my clients make such meaningful transitions.

The most successful corporate executives I have met surround themselves with colleagues who have strengths in the areas they need development, which includes specific areas of EQ. They also continue to challenge themselves to stretch outside their own comfort zone and to practise the skill areas they need to improve on. Of course, they will never be perfect in all areas. However, with a high level of self-awareness and an understanding of how their behaviour impacts others, they can do a superb job as a leader and role model. They understand how the different styles and strengths of their people enrich their overall team to maximize the potential of each team member. This helps retain top talent and positively impacts productivity and profits. It may feel counterintuitive, but the reality is that the higher you move in the leadership ranks, the more important your interpersonal behaviour becomes. At lower levels of leadership, brilliant contributors with great technical skills can produce results. The more senior your position, the more leadership is about "them" and less about "you."

Daniel Goleman, Richard Boyatzis, and Annie McKee summarize it this way: "No creature can fly with just one wing.

Gifted leadership occurs where heart and head — feeling and thought — meet. These are the two wings that allow a leader to soar.... Intellect alone will not make a leader; leaders execute a vision by motivating, guiding, inspiring, listening, persuading — and, most crucially, through creating resonance. As Albert Einstein cautioned, 'We should take care not to make the intellect our god. It has, of course, powerful muscles, but no personality. It cannot lead, it can only serve.'"[11]

4. Negotiating and Conflict Management

Every executive knows that conflict and disagreements in organizations and teams are inevitable and, for the most part, healthy. That is why it is so essential for exceptional leaders to build their competence for problem-solving, influencing, negotiating, and dealing with conflict and confrontation. An executive who is highly skilled in these areas has one of the most effective tools a leader can use to transform organizational objectives into desired outcomes.

Successful executives respect and anticipate that conflicts will happen often. They welcome and encourage positive conflict — that's what generates great ideas, insights, and "whole brain" thinking for outstanding decision-making. They understand that everyone is unique with very different points of view. As a result, executives often have to resolve conflicts. In some ways, this is a good thing! The value of conflict is that it forces us to identify issues, thoroughly look at pros and cons, and explore new alternatives. Successful executives need to be well-equipped and prepared to deal with conflict on a daily basis in a healthy way, while understanding that the overall goal is success for the team and organization to move forward.

Unfortunately, some executives are overly focused on their own popularity and acceptance, and they fear conflict and confrontation. They tend to surround themselves with "yes-people," staff who always tell them exactly what they want to hear. This gives executives a false sense of security, so that they appear to be an excellent leader. However, in today's business world, this can be a very risky approach for an executive. If the executive's staff or team member is not comfortable to speak up or share candid information about a potential problem that could interfere with the success of the team or the department, this can negatively impact both the executive and the organization. That's why the wise executive understands that encouraging healthy conflict and being approachable — conflict or no conflict — is a distinct advantage as a leader.

While some executives try to avoid conflict by surrounding themselves with compliant staff who may be afraid to speak up, other executives try to avoid conflict because they perceive conflict as creating winners and losers. However, when effectively managed, conflict allows there to be winners on both sides of the conflict, as well as from both the individual and the organizational viewpoint. Successful executives know how to get beyond the idea that it is important for them to be right. Their role is to ensure that the organization is making the right decision by working with their teams.

Managing conflict is often difficult. But successful executives understand that behaviours and attitudes like intimidation, arrogance, disrespect, raising your voice, and showing a temper are simply unacceptable. If executives do fall into one of these traps, others in their team, their organization, or their clients will quickly lose respect for them, and respect is a fundamental quality underlying exceptional leadership. Today's employees, brought up in the Generation X and Generation Y eras, were typically raised in an environment where they were listened to and respected for their opinion. They will not tolerate intimidation, arrogance, or disrespect for long. Bright successful executives today understand too well that the high costs of retaining top talent and finding new talent demands zero tolerance of disrespectful or intimidating behaviour.

Successful executive leaders maintain the attitude that in a potential conflict situation, they will most likely learn something new, rather than assume they will disagree. Rather than intimidation and arrogance, they practise other basic skills like being patient, speaking clearly and slowly, actively listening, and asking key questions to ensure that they know where the other person is coming from. Getting the facts and concerns on the table to make the best decisions are good indicators that they are mastering the skill of conflict management.

So much of being successful in business is about relationships. That is why it is critical not to take things for granted — especially if there appears to be conflict or concerns. Great leaders always ask questions and get regular feedback from their boss and others in their team. This feedback may be through a two-way conversation, or candid feedback from colleagues, team members, staff, or major customers, as well as 360 Feedback results.

Leaders with integrity always feel confident enough to express their views, even if their views may cause conflict. They demonstrate consistent behaviour. They want to be sure others know who they are, what they stand for, and what their expectations are. Conversations with honesty and integrity always lead to more meaningful discussions that can enhance clarity and assist in decision-making — especially around resolving conflicts.

Negotiating skills are closely linked to conflict management. Negotiation involves reaching an agreement with another person or group on a mutually acceptable course of action. To do this, leaders use influence. Often, a scenario begins with the executive influencing his boss, staff, peers, or a client to more deeply understand business-related issues. He communicates to persuade others to buy in to his perspective on the subject matter and to gather support to move forward in the direction he would like the team to go in achieving the desired outcomes of the organization. In a one-on-one situation, when two parties agree, there is automatic acceptance from both parties to move forward smoothly. When the two parties don't agree, it takes more energy and effort to discuss and influence the other party. In some cases, they may "agree to disagree." However, when the issue requires the agreement of both parties to move forward, the next step is to negotiate how to move forward together with a fair deal for both parties. The executive attempts to reach a mutually accepted course of action with the other person, team, or group. Sometimes the negotiating process becomes more challenging and there's no agreement. Negotiating almost always presupposes conflict. In other words, if there is no resolution in the negotiating, the next step is conflict management.

Let me give you an example of how excellent negotiation skills can help executives maximize their performance. I provided executive coaching services to a group of 15 executive-level general managers from across North America. The interesting pattern was that most of them were incredibly frustrated having such a large number of defined objectives on their plate. In many cases, as leaders, they were responsible for 15 to 20 major objectives. What a way to set up high-performing executives for failure! To achieve success, executives need to ensure they negotiate with CEOs to achieve three to five strategic objectives, not 15 to 20. With a handful of major objectives, executives and high-potential leaders are streamlined and focused on what really matters for both themselves and the organization. As a result, when they have the courage to negotiate these terms as an individual or group, and are successful in reducing the larger number of objectives to three to five major ones with huge impact, they perform better, accomplish more, and move their organization forward to more significant gains in productivity and profits. Instead of feeling over-committed and under-satisfied, they can achieve extraordinary success in their personal and organizational life.

For the most part, most of the conflicts with corporate executives I've coached over the years relate to differences in managerial and behaviourial styles in their team as well as lack of communication and listening skills. This reinforces the critical importance of the strong message throughout this book that to be successful, executives need to have a high level of self-awareness and an understanding of how their behaviour impacts others.

For example, one of my coaching clients, a VP of marketing, was highly stressed in managing his team of eight because two of his team members were consistently in conflict. He tried a variety of scenarios when setting up team members to work on different projects. However, no matter what arrangements he tried to engineer, it didn't seem to make a difference. Whenever these two team members worked together, they were always in conflict. Of course, this was reducing the overall productivity of the team.

The VP was a very proactive and results-oriented individual with a strong desire to move forward in achieving his desired objectives. Interestingly, he had excellent relationships with the two team members in conflict, let's call them Tom and Cathy. They were both skilled and savvy enough to "manage-up" to the boss and meet his particular needs. There is often more of a natural incentive to manage-up, as the boss usually has more clout over an individual's performance review and rewards than their peers. However, despite their good relationship with their boss, Tom and Cathy often disagreed with each other. They would attempt to persuade the VP to prefer their opinion or reasoning on different matters related to projects.

To address the conflict and strengthen the team, we assessed the managerial/behaviourial styles of both the VP and his eight team members. By learning more about the group as a whole, the VP could focus legitimately on the areas of strength of each team member, as well as learn more about specific areas for their development. Although there are levels of complexity to in-depth assessments, for the purpose of this example I will focus on the predominant differences. One major difference that came to the surface through the team assessment was that Tom was very extraverted and Cathy was very introverted. Tom often felt that Cathy was not fully co-operating when they worked on joint projects. He would wait for her to give him research and data and felt she was not meeting his expected timelines. On the other hand, Cathy felt that Tom was interrupting her work flow by constantly asking her questions about the project. Sometimes he asked the same questions several times, even though she had taken the time to respond and explain the answers in detail. As a result of the lack of understanding about each other's managerial and behaviour styles, there was constant stress between them. They would end up in conflict over and over again.

The team-based intervention was a rich learning process for the VP and each of the eight team members, especially for Tom and Cathy. Everyone learned more about how the different managerial/behaviourial styles can enrich the entire team. They also learned that for outstanding "whole brain" thinking and decision making, it is behaviours demonstrated by team members with different styles that bring the richness to the overall decision-making process.

Within a short period of time, Tom and Cathy were no longer in conflict. In fact, they had learned how best to use each other as a resource, helping each other in the skill areas that were not their own preference. They had enhanced their self-awareness and further understood how their behaviour impacted others. Further, the VP was now able to better understand how Tom and Cathy's characteristics and strengths could better contribute to the team's overall decision making. A few weeks later, the team met with their advertising agency to prepare for the launch of a new product. The VP and team were not only energized by the excitement of the new product, the whole team was highly engaged in taking their relationship skills to a whole new level as a team.

The key lesson here was that the VP approached the issue of managing conflict in a way that resulted in both resolving the conflict among the two staff members and, at the same time, enriching the relationships of all team members. As a result, the VP was able to enhance overall group decision-making. And he was able to further capitalize on the strengths and productivity of the team members to achieve even greater results for the marketing department of the organization.

5. Managing Energy and Time

Time is an irreplaceable commodity. A precious treasure, and a matchless gift. No matter how wealthy, creative, or connected we are, we cannot buy it, manufacture it, or produce more than 24 hours of it in a single day. What we can do, however, is adjust how we use the time we have control over, and how we manage our energy and time. Just as health is your wealth, time is your life.

Many top-level executives have attended workshops and seminars on time management, and have read books on the importance of good planning, being organized, prioritizing tasks, and so on. Most often, it's not that we lack information on what is required to have a better balance of wellness in our lives (i.e., good nutrition, exercise, a good night's sleep, etc.), it's mostly about how we prioritize our lives. There is an unmistakable link between achieving extraordinary success and how executives use their time. And, there are a number of excellent resources available on the topic. Sifting through it all and drawing on my experience with hundreds of corporate executives, I have discovered one fundamental principle that, if given attention and growth, means big wins for executives. Excellent leaders practise and master this principle of managing energy and time and, as a result, set themselves up for extraordinary success in both their personal and organizational lives. The principle is: stay laser-focused on what matters most.

The successful executive understands that managing energy and time is about making wise choices about their personal and organizational lives. They know how important it is to align their personal vision and values with their short- and long-term personal and organizational objectives. They understand the power of exceptional leadership and the undeniable importance of wellness and work/life balance. They choose actions that honour their most important priorities. They respect that time is precious and they spend it on what matters most in their personal and professional life.

An executive's list of projects and activities in both their professional and personal lives can be never ending. However, when I facilitate the process for executives to discover their personal vision, they get so laser-focused on what matters most in their personal and professional lives, that at least 30 percent of the original projects and activities are qualified as a poor use of time. It's like a fresh start — a major turn-around. All of a sudden, they have all this available time that was filled up with things that were not directly aligned with what mattered most, and they now have more time to focus on what does. Many executives excel in coming up with ideas and concepts, and they have great intentions to execute them. However, the exceptional executive knows that what gets scheduled is what gets done. Ideas need to be planned, broken into steps, and scheduled in order to be executed.

The more executives stay focused on what really matters in their lives, the easier it is for them to remove non-essential projects from their agendas. This often leads to eliminating other clutter, like surplus possessions they no longer use or need, and things that do not enhance their life. Successful executives know that there is power in the principle that less is more, and they experience what I call "the luxury of simplicity."

How well do you balance what's important to you with what is urgent to others? Consider reviewing a few projects that you are currently undertaking. Imagine a scale of one to 10, with "what matters least" at one end and "what matters most" at the other. Where along this scale would you rate the importance of a particular project to what really matters in your life?

Exceptional leaders always follow through on matters of importance and commitments they make. The wise executive understands that there is much leverage in simply following through. They easily build huge credibility with peers, staff, and clients. They instinctively imply that they are reliable, dependable, and very highly committed to aligning vision, leadership, and wellness in the organization. Following through also demonstrates respect to others and fosters a healthy learning environment for employees. Again, it's about Choice, Courage, and Commitment.

Not only do exceptional leaders stay laser-focused on what matters most to them as mapped out in their personal vision, they make sure their energy and time at work is aligned with organizational objectives.

One of my good friends is a top-level executive with a major automobile manufacturer. She knows that you can either spend time, or invest time. Every day, she asks herself, "What is the return on investment for me and my organization in terms of how I spent my day?" While some activities have a relatively low return on investment, they are facts of life within a corporation and need to be done. However, we must be careful to minimize the amount of time we spend on such activities. For example, the successful executive never plans a meeting to solve a problem that can easily be addressed by an email or conference call. Having 10 people at a meeting can be extremely costly to any organization. The next time you are at a meeting, count the number of attendees. If you know their approximate hourly salaries, you can add up the true cost of that meeting. You will quickly understand why it is essential for each meeting to be highly productive to resolve issues within the meeting timelines. Exceptional leaders ensure that their time at work is invested in activities that achieve organizational objectives and results.

Highly skilled executives find ways to complete a day's work within the workday. They are absolutely brilliant. They have the confidence and courage to negotiate three to five major objectives that can have a significant impact on the bottom line of the organization. They also know when to delegate and outsource projects to prevent burnout to themselves and their staff. It is an exceptional case, not regular practice, for them to work overtime. Leaders who delegate and develop others for succession planning positions are also making wise choices about how they use their own time. They can complete their own projects, while also providing support and project development opportunities for others. They are also exceptional role models for their team.

Years ago, the company star was often the workaholic who spent 16 hours a days at the office even though they were exhausted. They negatively impacted morale at work and were less productive in the long term. The company star today — especially in progressive organizations — is the leader who is competent, confident, and inspires others by his example of balancing his work and non-work activities to be a consistent high performer. Successful executives know that whether it is themselves or the staff they are leading, overwork can lead to short- and long-term sickness and disability expenses for the organization — a "no win" situation for both the employee and the organization.

What specific things do highly successful executives do to manage their time wisely? They are highly disciplined. They know the times of the day and week when they are most alert and productive. They understand that perseverance and following through are key to their credibility and respect, and essential to their life and career. They wisely consider whether they are focused on the right activities. If something is on their list of projects or activities, it must be aligned in some way with what is important for them to achieve in their bigger picture. Are you a procrastinator? Most executives who achieve extraordinary success are not procrastinators. Many of my coaching clients have been surprised to discover the link between procrastination and their lack of clear personal vision. Once you discover what keeps you anchored in your personal vision and how far away from it you are willing to venture, it will further clarify your priorities, and naturally motivate you toward higher performance.

Successful executives schedule "think time" regularly on their calendar to reflect on the status of their objectives and how these can be streamlined and best accomplished. They trust their inner wisdom in making tough choices and have the courage to say "no" when it's required. Although many are highly driven and can be perfectionists, they understand that things do not always go as planned. As much as they want to achieve their desired results within short timelines, they try not to over-schedule. They leave a buffer for emergencies. Wise executives are careful about what they include on their calendars in the first place. Most highly successful executives are very committed to what they promise others, and themselves. They understand that when they make a commitment to an organization, staff, friend, family, partner, or themselves, they must follow through. Not following through naturally creates more stress for them, and after a while can take a toll on the health of the body.

We live in a world where multi-tasking has become the norm. However, although it may appear that multi-taskers are achieving much more, they are often simply rushing through a variety of tasks that consistently interrupt their thought processes. Another major negative implication of multi-tasking is increased human error. Over the last decade, more and more serious incidents and accidents have occurred in numerous industries as a result of people trying to multi-task instead of giving important matters their full attention. Although you may find this surprising, my experience is that, for the most part, highly successful executives do not multi-task. Top-level executives have a number of priorities that demand their focus at any one time. However, the approach of exceptional leaders is to apply themselves to a single task without interruption, complete that segment, and then move on to something else. They do not allow an array of communication and high-technology gadgets to vie for their attention. They respect the high-tech tools and use them when appropriate, for practical use and not prestige. But they clearly understand that the brain can only handle one thing well at a time, and that energy and time wasted in multi-tasking is lost forever. Research is increasingly showing that instant email alerts on devices like computers, BlackBerrys, or iPhones actually inhibit productivity, particularly visual alerts. Instead, exceptional top-level executives wisely turn off their alerts, or at the very least, only use alerts for those key contacts needed to accomplish their daily objectives. If you added up the time required in just one day to constantly shift or refocus your attention on a number of different tasks, you would be surprised at the cumulative total. It makes sense that uni-tasking yields higher performance.

Even though most highly successful executives do not multi-task, they are still highly effective at making their time available to others when it is aligned with their objectives and is the right thing to do. When they meet with someone, they ensure that they give them their undivided attention at that appointed time. By demonstrating respect to the individual, they naturally build the relationship, and more easily achieve the desired outcome of the meeting.

Often, getting a new grip on managing energy and time and becoming laser-focused on what matters most means finding a new balance in our lives. Just like the earth has a natural rhythm, so does our body. The sun rises, the sun sets, the moon rises, the moon sets. The tides come in, the tides go out. When our schedules get out of whack, we need to slow our lives down and find our own natural rhythms again. Like the ocean, we have a natural rhythm or pace that feels and works best for us. Getting back in balance usually involves regaining control of your time by being proactive instead of reactive, scheduling time for yourself in your planner, and simplifying your life. It may even eventually involve changing jobs, downsizing to a smaller home, or moving. But it's a process, not an event.

Successful executives recognize that spending 10 to 15 percent more of their time on a strong outside interest or family time can mean the difference between success and failure. In fact, it provides greater balance in their lives, and can often create extraordinary success for both the executive and the organization. Feelings of guilt in missing a son's baseball game or a daughter's dance recital become big regrets over time, because that time is lost forever. In the later years of life, these regrets can deepen into guilt, as children marry and have grandchildren. Executives need to know their choices mattered. Once again, what is your personal vision and how does it all fit together for you?

Many of the executives I coach are amazed once they understand the importance of making their self-care a priority. Initially, some view this as selfishness. By the third coaching session, they realize that by taking extra time for their own self-care, they are able to give so much more to both their family and their organization. The bonus is that they accomplish more by expending less energy. Remember, every day that goes by is another day that you will never get back. So make the best of your day by focusing on what matters most.

Launched in 2006, *The Dash* movie, at *www.thedashmovie. com*, has been watched by millions of people worldwide. Using a series of still photographs and simple text, the movie reminds us that the dash — that small bit of punctuation on a tombstone between the date of birth and the date of our death — is what matters.

Try this powerful exercise. Take out a piece of paper and draw a horizontal line that begins with your birth and ends with your death. How far are you along the line? What do you need and want to do before the end? For some, this exercise helps put your life in perspective, especially when you think about where, how, and with whom you spend your time.

How will you spend your dash? We never know how long it will be. Ask yourself, are my priorities where they should be? Am I spending my time on what matters most?

Executives who have defined their personal vision have an edge for themselves, their families, their teams, and their organizations. They naturally see the bigger picture, and how their energy and time between home life and work life need to be managed. Managing their priorities becomes simpler and easier. This naturally allows them to be even more disciplined in carrying out their key accountabilities in the organization. This is part of the magic allowing them to align their vision, leadership, and wellness to achieve extraordinary success.

Do you know what matters most for you? Does the way you invest your energy and time reflect those priorities? Highly successful corporate executives understand that although time often means money, by taking the proper time to develop a solid personal and organizational vision, much time is actually saved over the long term. They get it right the first time. They understand how important it is for them to spend their time doing what matters most for them. In their later years, they can look back to what they did with their lives, and with whom they spent their valuable time, with a great feeling of accomplishment.

They keep in mind that it's always about the journey, not the destination. They stay focused on what matters most.

6. Mastering Lifestyle Management and Overall Wellness

It may seem bold to include mastering lifestyle management and overall wellness as the sixth key leadership competency. However, working alongside hundreds of corporate executives over the years and coaching them to peak performance has proven over and over again that this key leadership competency is critical. Plain and simple, it works! In fact, this competency is most often the missing piece executives need to achieve and sustain extraordinary success, especially in the fast-paced business world of the twenty-first century. You can have all of the other five key leadership competencies, but if you are missing number six, you are at a major disadvantage.

Mastering lifestyle management and overall wellness is the true edge for the executive. Leaders who master this competency understand that being healthy and having a high level of energy positively impacts productivity and profits for themselves, and for their staff, team, and organization. Much of my coaching practice is about working with executives to discover what works best for them to have a better balance in life and a better quality of life from a wellness perspective, both personally and professionally. Once they find this balance, they are well on their way to living the life of their dreams.

What does mastering lifestyle management and overall wellness mean? Firstly, it means that the executive needs to be in control of managing his or her own personal lifestyle and overall wellness, including developing a solid reserve of resilience. Secondly, it means the executive needs to be a leader and role model in doing so for others.

Lifestyle management and personal wellness are life skills; we don't learn them in school, yet they are critical for our health and wellbeing. What I want to highlight is translating these life skills into a leadership skill. As a corporate executive or high-potential leader, an important part of your job is to be a leader for your team and your organization on lifestyle management and overall wellness. You do not need to know everything about lifestyle management and wellness to be a leader in this area, but you do have to have a good handle on your own lifestyle management and overall wellness. With your own experience, and as role model for others, you are more equipped to be compassionate and make the most appropriate decisions for your staff, department, division, and organization.

For executive leaders, mastering wellness and lifestyle management means not only the ability to maintain a healthy mind and body, it also means having a reserve of resilience that you can access when required to consistently maintain your energy levels. Developing a solid reserve of resilience is always a great competitive edge over other corporate executives. Like a palm tree bending in a storm, strengthening its root system at the same time, the resilient executive rebounds stronger than ever to the challenges. The ideal situation is to sustain optimal performance by ensuring that you can get time out to re-energize when you need it and avoid burnout from ever happening. Why? Because when burnout occurs, it is too late; the damage is already done.

Mastering lifestyle and overall wellness competency is multi-faceted. It includes not only your professional work, but all of the other areas outside of work including health, finances, social relationships, and so on. Executives needs to ensure that they are managing their energy and time in such a way that they're paying sufficient attention to all aspects of their personal and professional lives. These areas will be covered more deeply in the personal wellness section of this book. When the executive's work or life becomes too challenging, he or she needs to make adjustments to their priorities. An executive may need to let go of some things that are not as important as others in order to refocus priorities and achieve a better balance. When executives have a high level of self-awareness, and are honest with themselves about the reality of their situation and challenges, they can easily recognize what's happening before becoming overwhelmed. That's the time to make the adjustments: well before burnout.

When executives have not mastered their own lifestyle management and overall wellness, they often feel overwhelmed or frustrated. They have trouble sleeping at night and some suffer from insomnia. They may experience unusual outbreaks of anger. They may get sick or experience sudden changes in how their body feels overall. They may be significantly overweight or underweight, both of which greatly stress the body and their health in the long term. They may experience signs of burnout. In a nutshell, they simply lack wellness. This puts them at a disadvantage, because if they can't be in control of mastering their own personal lifestyle management and overall wellness, it's very difficult for them to lead others in this competency area.

Making wise decisions related to lifestyle management, as well as work/life balance, for unusual staff requests and unexpected incidents can be very tough. Today's challenges are difficult and complex, and there are few case studies to refer to on some of these topics. In fact, many of the problems that executives face require making decisions on issues that never existed before. Think about the technological revolution. In less than a decade, technology has connected every human being on the planet. The impact on industries, organizations, executives, and staff has major implications for global organizations and the executives that run them. However, even in tough times, exceptional leaders are able to keep their focus and readily adapt to change.

Decision making for the leader in this competency area usually relates to addressing staff issues at the same time as meeting commitments to complete key projects related to the strategic business plan. Let me explain. As a role model of lifestyle management and overall wellness, exceptional leaders are committed to managing not only their team's performance, but also their team's work/life balance. Imagine you are rolling out a new product in the current quarter. In the midst of the project, you have a top notch product manager who wants to go on sabbatical to fulfill a dream of completing a triathlon. Or a key employee suddenly needs to move an elderly parent into her home and needs time to make the adjustment. Or an outstanding employee shares that the challenges of looking after his autistic son is affecting his work and he needs more time at home. All of these examples involve delicate decisions on the executive's part related to his or her staff's lifestyle management and overall wellness, as well as retaining top talent.

Decision making around these kinds of issues are often escalated to the executive level because the employee may have highly technical expertise that is difficult to find elsewhere. The consequences of not having that skill available for the organization may be the "make it or break it" point for fulfilling a key area of major accountability related to the strategic business plan. Some decisions you make as a leader and as a role model can have huge long term impact on the organization.

After the 9/11 terrorist attacks, some of my executives shared with me that several of their highly valuable employees were adamant against taking any flights for months after the event. What would you do? These are not easy decisions to make, especially when you are confident that you already employ staff who are the best talent around and you need them to be fully committed to meeting their professional objectives.

Whether the challenges around lifestyle management involve pursuing exciting ventures, dealing with family illness, skills shortages, or other issues, executives have these challenges consistently on their plate. What is key is that decisions need to be fair and reasonable for both parties to retain that top talent, especially because the decisions often fall outside established organizational policies and procedures. It is costly to find new talent and bring them up to speed to complete key projects on time. Keep in mind, what is at stake relates to your commitment, credibility, and accountability for achieving the key objectives of your portion of the strategic business plan. Executives need to weigh the sacrifices and consequences of decisions that are connected to lifestyle management and overall wellness aspects for their staff. The challenge, for the executive and his department, is to deal with the short-term issues around lifestyle management and work/life balance, while still achieving outstanding results for the organization and in keeping with the organization's values and corporate guidelines. That requires an executive who is both compassionate and responsive, who has a solid grip on his own lifestyle management and wellness, and can make the best decision for the employee, the department, and the organization in keeping with corporate guidelines.

Of course, the wise executive, director, or manager will initially get consultation and counsel from human resources related to these lifestyle issues for staff. Most likely, your organization has services and information available — for example, through the Employee Assistance Program — that can help with issues such as elder care, home care, counselling, and so on. However, in the end you are the decision maker. You were hired as the director or vice-president to lead and manage your department, not human resources. Line management is responsible for all the results of their department or division.

Because of the ongoing challenges and complexities of these decisions, executives need to have some high quality downtime to "clear the cobwebs." This involves time away or on their own to digest the different strategies to cover all the options and make the best decision for the organization. For many executives, speakers, and executive coaches, including myself, time away from work can also have surprising links to how we make our money. Why? Because it is often when we are relaxed — working out, playing a sport, walking the beach, having a shower, or out sailing — that our leading-edge ideas come to us. That is why it is always important to have pen and paper handy to capture and record our incredible insights before we forget them. The insights that come to us when we have the right amount of space and balance in our lives can be the true difference in moving an organization forward, addressing a lifestyle management issue with a team member, finding a more creative way to deal with a challenge with a customer, or getting an audience's attention in the introduction of a presentation. When we are away from work and our mind is totally relaxed and filled with oxygen, walking along the beach or in the forest, amazing insights happen.

Taking care of yourself first and being in control of mastering your own personal lifestyle management and overall wellness is the first step to providing leadership and being a role model — and this links right back to your personal vision. Let me tell you about Mary, a single mother of two teenaged daughters. Mary is an executive I worked with a few years ago who wanted to focus on developing her leadership competency of mastering overall wellness and lifestyle management. Together, we developed a customized coaching plan that began with clarifying her personal vision, and moved into maximizing her performance and creating a better balance. As a result of our process, she sold her large home with a huge pool, since she and her daughters were seldom home to enjoy it. That allowed her to purchase her dream cottage 10 years earlier than she thought was possible; she also bought a small townhouse in the city as her daughters went off to university. She was able to continue to perform her position as a vice-president of sales much closer to her home in the northern part of United States. The quality of her personal life allowed her much more time for herself and her daughters. That was positively reflected in her improved organizational performance results. In fact, she was the only vice-president of sales to exceed her quota the year she made these significant changes. In addition, she had more time for social life and met the man of her dreams. Her children have now graduated and she has a great life with her new husband. Over a short period of time, by having her own lifestyle management and overall wellness under control, she became much more confident and compassionate in demonstrating this key leadership competency for her staff and organization. She is a role model. She had developed a reserve of resilience, she "walks the talk," and she's achieving extraordinary success.

Unfortunately, only a small number of excellent role models demonstrate this sixth key leadership competency as Mary does. An exceptional executive must develop, practise, and be a role model and leader in mastering lifestyle management and wellness for his team, staff, and others in the organization.

UNDERSTANDING YOUR STRENGTHS
AND AREAS FOR GROWTH

In summary, exceptional leaders cultivate a high level of self-awareness through both formal and informal feedback. They have a realistic view of how they stack-up against the six key leadership competency areas for extraordinary success. Whether it is strategic thinking, communication and active listening, emotional intelligence, negotiating and conflict management, managing energy and time, or mastering lifestyle management and overall wellness, they know their areas of strengths *and* the areas they need to grow. They are excellent role models for their team, and in practising their leadership-skill areas, they strengthen team effectiveness. They continually work on further developing their leadership competencies, often with the assistance of an executive coach. Furthermore, they work with their coach to ensure their areas of focus for development are clearly linked to their personal performance and their contributions to the organization. When personal leadership is aligned with organizational leadership, built on the foundation of personal and organizational vision, and sustained and strengthened by personal and organizational wellness, that's The All Together Now Advantage, and that is when individuals and organizations achieve extraordinary success.

CHAPTER FOUR

Organizational Leadership

BEYOND PERSONAL LEADERSHIP TO ORGANIZATIONAL LEADERSHIP

I have met executives with great skills as personal leaders. Many have the ability to think strategically and communicate well. Their emotional intelligence may be high, and they may be adept at conflict management and negotiation. They may even be managing their energy and time according to the priorities of what matters most, living healthy lives, and practising wellness. However, these great personal leadership skills will not profoundly influence the organization they work for, unless executives cultivate not only their personal leadership, but their organizational leadership. Organizational leadership means putting those personal leadership skills into action in the context of the organization. Exceptional leaders of organizations understand where their organization needs to go to continue to grow in terms of creativity and innovation, revenues, customer satisfaction, employee satisfaction, and shareholder satisfaction.

Personal vision is about understanding your own purpose, passion, and values. Personal leadership begins with self-awareness and an understanding of how your behaviour impacts others, including your clients, your team, and other staff. Both are prerequisites for executives to be high performers and significantly contribute to organizational leadership. Why? Because solid personal vision and outstanding personal leadership skills greatly assist the executive in making the right choices. And it is the right choices that make a huge impact on achieving better results. Better results mean more profits for the organization, and greater gratification on the job for the executive. In so many cases, we are as successful as our choices. One of the most important themes for me in my coaching practice is the three Cs: Choice, Courage, and Commitment. From an organizational perspective, the more that senior management executives make solid choices with good judgment, are courageous enough to deal with the tough issues in the early stages, and are excellent models of commitment, the greater the chances for the organization to move forward in achieving their overall objectives. And when it comes to leadership, it's not only about demonstrating commitment, it's about fostering staff commitment.

Warren Bennis, a pioneer in the contemporary field of leadership studies, writes, "If I've learned anything from my research, it is this: The factor that empowers the work force and ultimately determines which organizations succeed or fail is the leadership of those organizations.... Leaders are people who do the right thing; managers are people who do things right."[1]

My experience coaching hundreds of executives over the past two decades, is that most organizations are managed, not led. Warren Bennis and Burt Nanus echo that perspective. They write, "The distinctive role of leadership is the quest for 'know why' ahead of 'know-how'... By focusing attention on a vision, the leader operates on the emotional and spiritual resources of the organization, on its values, commitment, and aspirations.

The manager, by contrast, operates on the physical resources of the organization; on its capital, human skills, raw materials and technology."[2] There are leaders and there are managers. Thriving organizations need both.

Organizational leadership is the place where executives put their personal leadership skills into action. This chapter will talk about why and how.

THE TWO PILLARS OF ORGANIZATIONAL LEADERSHIP

Extraordinary organizational leadership is built on two strong pillars — strategic business planning and succession planning. These two pillars are the spheres where executives need to walk the talk of their personal leadership skills in order to be highly effective in their organization.

The strategic business plan is developed from the organizational vision, values, and mission, and incorporates both the operational plans for the organization and the succession planning: talent management. In short, extraordinary success happens in organizations that have highly talented staff applying their outstanding skills by executing the plans of the organization to maximize productivity and profits in the organization. These highly successful organizations continually develop staff and teams to keep the momentum for the future success of the organization. To say it simply, the strategic business plan is the what (*what needs to happen*), and succession planning is the who (*who will do it*), for today and tomorrow.

The key focus for an organizational leader is to ensure that the organization continuously re-invents itself to take optimum advantage of new market opportunities. That's thinking and acting strategically. The leader's second priority is to ensure that the appropriate talent is selected, internally or externally, to develop and implement the vision. On average, only 5 percent

105

of the corporations listed on the Fortune 500 typically succeed in surviving on the list for more than 50 years. That is mainly because most organizations are populated with managers, not leaders and, as a consequence, they fail to ensure that the organization continuously recreates itself.

Outstanding executives use their leadership and influence to get others to buy into the direction the organization wants to go. Ultimately, it is the people and teams within the organization who make the strategic business plan happen. Succession planning also supports a major part of the execution of the strategic business plan — having the right person in the right job at the right time to maintain momentum, productivity, and profits for the organization. For organizations that achieve extraordinary success, the executive team will not only meet, but exceed organizational objectives. Personal leadership skills, acted out in the organization, positively impact results both directly and indirectly.

The real test happens when you see what behaviours are exhibited by executives at critical decision-making points. Highly successful executives are excellent role models for their team, demonstrating and applying their skills to lead, coach, and develop their staff. To be highly effective, they need to demonstrate the true vision and values of the organization to all employees. Organizational vision and values are simply words; the rubber really hits the road in how these executives and leaders act and interact in their day-to-day business environment as they bring the vision and values to life.

Achieving extraordinary success takes practice. Conventional wisdom is that it takes about 10,000 hours of practice to become an expert. Whether it's sports or leadership, practice helps champions rise to the challenge. Watch tennis professionals like Roger Federer or Rafael Nadal. When under pressure, they change their tactics, making it extremely challenging for the other person. They shift to different strategies with ease, because they have practised each of them so often. The 1980s tennis-great Bjorn Borg had a philosophy for tennis that was simple: "I win the match by getting one more ball back than the other guy." In a way, that is what organizational leadership is all about: being better than the competition. If each leader and their team can demonstrate solid leadership skills under pressure, they have a huge edge over the competition to achieve outstanding results for the organization.

Strategic business planning and succession planning are the two critical pillars of organizational leadership, and the necessary architecture for extraordinary organizational success. This chapter examines both of these pillars, providing insights that have the potential to transform your organization, and your role and practice as a senior-level executive or high-potential leader.

EIGHT KEY COMPONENTS OF A HIGH IMPACT STRATEGIC PLANNING PROCESS

Strategic planning is the process used by senior management to jointly define and envision the overall strategies of the organization for future growth, and to develop specific and necessary strategies, procedures, and operations to achieve that future.

In my coaching practice, I am completely committed to a whole system approach to strategic business planning, a method that embraces and aligns the entire system of an organization's activities. I also believe it is critically important that the strategy be easily understood by all managers to create a high level of engagement to implement the plan.

There is an abundance of standard tools and analytical frameworks used in strategic planning. However, most of them are focused on using the competition as a benchmark. In order not to let existing market structure limit people's thinking, I believe it's important to focus on the broader potential of expanding existing markets and exploring untapped markets to seize new growth opportunities.

As someone who has facilitated hundreds of strategic business plans for organizations, I've learned that asking the right questions at the right time is critical. In the end, senior team leaders have to be absolutely clear on their specific areas of accountability. Each senior team member needs to be highly engaged in accelerating the plan to achieve the desired outcomes. The final step is for the organization to implement and execute the plan with a focus on solid team leadership and individual accountability.

A high impact strategic planning process is illustrated below.

There are eight key components:

1. Formulate and/or update the vision, mission, and core values
2. Develop a customized strategic planning model
3. Assess the competition and the market by examining in-depth the internal and external environment impacting the organization
4. Assess the organization "inwardly and outwardly"; a detailed Strength/Weakness/Opportunities/Threats (SWOT) analysis of the organization, including an assessment of the impact of social/economic trends, market/industry trends, regulatory activities, customer service relationships (CSR) issues, employment demographics, and trends on the organization and its products and services
5. Complete a performance audit linked to the succession planning process
6. Conduct a gap analysis
7. Complete the action plan, including a contingency plan
8. Implement the strategic business plan and measure progress.

If any of these key components are missing, the organization is unlikely to be highly effective at achieving extraordinary success. Getting the process done right takes skill and experience. An outstanding facilitator has the ability to quickly grasp and digest complex terminology, data, and information, and the wisdom to ensure the plan is written in a practical format. Regrettably, many outside consultants will come into an organization and take a laborious six months or more to complete the process. However, highly skilled facilitators know how to work closely with in-house expertise who are best positioned to gather information in a cost-effective way. Further, by asking the right questions, an outstanding facilitator can discern when the organization is best served by in-house expertise, and when they should outsource a request on a particular topic to gather leading-edge information from a research company. This can save the organization both time and money.

When the strategic planning process is completed effectively, often with the facilitation of an external coach, the direction for the organization is clearly articulated and identified from an operations perspective, and people and talent are linked together. The plan also includes the major organizational objectives and key measurements for the desired outcomes, with appropriate resources allocated. These organizational objectives are developed jointly by the CEO and the senior executive team. These objectives are then divided among the key divisions which have the technical and leadership skills to make it happen. Most of the work I do is with mid- and large-size organizations that already have basic job descriptions with key competencies, solid recruiting, and selection processes in place, and a performance management system. These are the fundamental requirements for supporting the strategic business plan.

Some organizations flounder during the process of creating a strategic business plan. They make it overly complex and months, and even years, may pass before they agree on a direction. By contrast, successful organizations get a solid strategic business plan done on an efficient timeline and utilize appropriate internal and external expertise. Then, as they say in broadcasting, they get on with the show.

It sounds relatively simple. But you may be wondering, if strategic business planning is so well documented, and if it can be so easily boiled down to eight key components, why do so many executives fumble instead of fly? I believe there are two main reasons. The first is that executives may be operating like lost sheep in an organization that simply does not have — or does not live out — a clearly defined organizational vision, mission, and set of core values married to a solid strategic business plan. And the second is that the strategic business plan may not be adequately linked to a performance measurement system with clear expectations and regular feedback. Let me expand on both of these reasons why executives and organizations falter instead of achieving extraordinary success.

The lost-sheep executive

I have met far too many executives who are in the stressful position of being lost sheep in their organization, wandering about lacking clear objectives, without expectations laid out in a solid strategic business plan.

When executives get a job offer for an exciting new senior-level position, they often instinctively know that one of the main reasons they were highly successful in their previous organization was because they had a solid strategic business plan. They use the strategic plan as a guide to stay on track toward achieving their objectives, demonstrating great leadership skills, and receiving their bonuses and excellent compensation. However, many of these executives do not put enough emphasis on ensuring that the organization they are joining has a solid organizational vision, mission, set of core values, strategic business plan, and succession planning process in place. If you want to achieve extraordinary success, this has to be a "deal breaker." Be sure to do your homework so you know whether or not the organization is just paying lip service to its commitment to all of these important building blocks; these elements are key factors to keeping you on track to achieve extraordinary success.

Of course, a new executive may be hired to fix a failed organization that suffered from a lack of strategic business planning in the first place. In this instance, the executive joining the organization should insist that a strategic business plan

111

activity be a first priority at the executive level, facilitated within the first three months of joining the senior executive team.

When there is no organizational vision, mission, or set of core values, there is no clear purpose or focus for the organization's existence. Without this foundation, and without a solid strategic business plan, it is also impossible to have an effective succession planning process. Operating without a solid strategic business plan also means that, although you may have operational numbers and targets, they are not connected to a performance management system with clear objectives linked to the strategic business plan. When that is your reality, the specific areas for achieving results become very grey for both the executive and the organization.

Fast forward to several months past the hiring process in the organization lacking focus. It is now time for the performance review of the executive, along with his or her annual increase with bonus. However, what has been achieved is fuzzy. At the time of the review, the executive and the boss tend to disagree on the exact accomplishments in view of their own personal perspectives about expectations. The excuse might be that they were both too busy to find time to meet more regularly to clarify the specific expectations or objectives. Without clarity, it is difficult to know how to specifically measure results and provide a proper performance rating. This kind of executive is like a lost sheep wandering in a misty meadow. They are not sure where they are going, and they certainly cannot assess or adequately demonstrate whether they have reached their destination. This has significant consequences, because the performance rating translates into the dollars paid out for their annual increase, bonus, stock options, and so on.

Fast forward again. Within a short period of time, the communication between the boss and the executive begins to erode and break down. More conflict begins to happen in a "you said, I said" scenario. The executive thinks he has overachieved.

The CEO believes the executive has underachieved in some areas of his objectives, and certainly hasn't exceeded in any. Who knows who's right? Probably no one, as measurable objectives and clear expectations related to productivity and profits for the organization were never part of a solid strategic business plan in the first place. The objectives were never formally set. And, as you know from the story of personal and organizational vision, trust is everything. Now trust has broken down.

Whose fault is it? We can safely say, both. However, keep in mind that executives who achieve extraordinary success, for the most part, go beyond the call of duty to over-prepare in researching and finding out as much as they can about an organization prior to joining it. Before accepting a job offer, they understand that this is their time to negotiate and set themselves up for success, while the hiring corporation still has a strong desire to buy their bag of skills.

These executives are adamant about knowing, seeing, and understanding the organization's vision and set of core values. They want to ensure that the organizational vision and values are in good alignment with their own personal vision. They also won't move forward in a final interview without being privy to at least the fundamentals of the organization's strategic business plan. This helps set them up for success from the beginning, as they can identify how they can use their leadership skills and technical knowledge to contribute to the development of people, productivity, and profits in the organization. From the start, they focus on three to five key objectives that are agreed upon by their future boss, the senior VP or CEO. They feel confident that, working effectively with their team, they can deliver on these objectives. And they ensure these objectives have specific and agreed-upon measurement terms. They are now set up for success — not failure.

When newly hired executives do not go through these steps, they will begin to recognize that their personal vision is out of sync with what is happening in the organization. They may no longer feel valued, as they are not using the skills they love in an environment that fosters positive learning, growth, and rewards. Both the executive and his or her boss might not be happy working together — or happy, period. After a while, the attitudes of both the executive and the boss naturally become more negative. This can also impact morale and productivity in the organization as it cascades down the levels of staff. The executive is dissatisfied. More conflicts are happening, and the executive recollects that this is not how they thought it would look six months or a year after being hired. By this time, their immune system begins to wear down. They are highly stressed and less motivated to do physical activities or work out. They don't sleep well at night, have less energy in the day, and get sick more easily. This cycle happens time and time again. And each time I see it, I come back again with renewed confidence in the incredible importance of aligning vision, leadership, and wellness to achieve extraordinary success.

What does success look like for you in your current organization, or the one you are joining? Are you a lost-sheep executive? Was it clear why you received, or did not receive, your last increase or bonus? If you didn't get it, it was likely a major challenge to prove you deserved it if you didn't have a clear set of objectives with proper measurement agreed upon in advance.

In my two and a half decades of experience coaching executives and providing consulting to organizations, I've learned that when executives have a strong handle on aligning their personal vision with the organizational vision and values, are highly skilled in their leadership abilities, practise wellness, *and* they have contributed to developing and implementing a solid strategic business plan, they are in the driver's seat. It is far easier for them to stay on track, achieve outstanding success, and even have more time for the leisure activities they love, things like golf, tennis, fitness, and relaxed time with the family.

Being highly committed to performance management

Another important component of the strategic business planning process is about doing it, and measuring it. Executives need to consistently measure the results achieved by their individual direct reports, as well as their overall team results. Formally, this process is called the performance management system. To keep it alive and highly effective, it requires ongoing communication and candid feedback throughout the year on what matters most to the individual and the organization.

With respect to personal leadership, it is the responsibility of the executive to proactively develop and nurture the skills of his or her team. The executive needs to be an excellent role model, mastering skills in strategic thinking, communication, negotiation and conflict management, emotional intelligence, managing time and energy, and mastering lifestyle management and overall wellness. In other words, top notch executives need to be practitioners who demonstrate the skills that they expect their direct reports and their team to develop and practise on an ongoing basis. Living out their vision, values, and skills is what gives executives credibility and authenticity with direct reports, peers, and other colleagues and customers.

Highly skilled executives will be committed to maximizing the use of the performance management system as an invaluable tool to stay on track and measure the performance of their direct reports, their team, and their own progress. This is best done by regularly asking the right questions and gathering feedback from staff and the team to ensure they are on track throughout the year.

Through a performance management review process, leaders jointly develop specific, measurable objectives, so both parties have clear expectations. If you are a top-notch leader or executive, you understand how directly the results of your staff can impact your own results. Therefore, wise executives are highly

115

committed to leading and coaching their team for outstanding results for themselves, their teams, and their organization.

Successful executives meet face-to-face twice a year or even quarterly to specifically measure progress, adjust objectives of staff where required, and provide additional candid feedback. There needs to be clear communication between the executive and the individual staff member and team so that all parties are clear on expectations. The overall aim here is to ensure there are never any surprises for the individual staff member regarding a performance rating, or overall team results.

In my experience, executives who have bosses who provide clear expectations, measurable objectives, and who follow up regularly, perceive their performance review as a great opportunity for feedback and growth. By contrast, where bosses do not practise this clarity around expectations and regular feedback, executives often perceive their performance review as a negative experience.

To get helpful and honest feedback, executives need to be approachable to their staff and team members. Remember: information is knowledge, and knowledge often includes exceptional ideas and concepts that can greatly build on growth and profit in the organization. Using their various emotional-intelligence competencies and the values of trust, humility, and respect, successful executives provide a learning environment that fosters a high comfort level where others can share their ideas. Staff will not share ideas with a boss who is not approachable, who lacks impulse control, who doesn't actively listen, and who does not give credit where credit is due. Consider this carefully, because a great idea from one of the staff on your team can be a breakthrough for your success, as well as the success of your team, your organization, and the shareholders of the organization.

Why do some executives flounder in their organizational leadership? Because they are not highly committed to a clear performance management system. And they do not request regular feedback from others on what matters most to them and their organization in terms of achieving the objectives of the strategic business plan.

WHO'S NEXT? THE PILLAR OF SUCCESSION PLANNING

In the realm of organizational leadership, strategic business planning is one of the two pillars for an organization to achieve extraordinary success. The other pillar is succession planning.

One of the major responsibilities of senior leaders is to ensure the organization has invested in the methods required to secure the talent pool necessary to sustain the organization in the long term. In other words, one of the most important parts of your job as an exceptional organizational leader is to make sure you have a potential successor in place.

Succession planning is a process that enables organizations to select, train, and develop staff — internally or externally — who can be available when a key position becomes vacant. This provides momentum and continuity to an organization, helping it achieve its short- and long-term corporate objectives. You could call it managing a just-in-time talent bank.

Just as organizations focus on today and tomorrow's products or services, their leaders have a responsibility to make sure their managerial talent is also able to manage current and future challenges. And, just as businesses and organizations need to account for their financial assets, they also need to account for their human assets. With the technology of today, most products are competitive; it's the human assets that differentiate one organization from another and make up the true leading edge of competition in the marketplace.

Exceptional personal leaders are continually mastering the skill of lifestyle management and overall wellness by investing attention in their personal, mental, and physical fitness to ensure continued success and effectiveness in the future. So also, organizations must take steps to ensure their continued wellness, especially from a leadership perspective. The basic challenge is to develop top leaders for their organization for both the short and the long term. To maintain their competitive edge, today's organizations need to be in the talent search and talent development business.

Recent statistics indicate that when there is no successor ready to replace an organization's president and CEO, the organization will experience a two-year period of lower profitability. Gallup polls tell us that up to 80 percent of workers are "disengaged" and circulating their résumés because their current organizations are not providing enough growth opportunities for leadership.

In today's fast-paced and changing business world, it is often difficult for executives to step away from the day-to-day operations to focus on developing the executive talent required to sustain and grow the organization for the future. Often, those who have been identified as future leaders will grow weary of waiting for an opportunity to assume more senior roles, and leave to join a competitor who can offer them the future today. That is why it's important to be sensitive to the timelines and commitments of succession planning and to groom several candidates for the same key position, or to assume multiple positions as required.

The goal of many progressive organizations is to provide an appropriate learning and development environment for a new, nimble, responsive-to-change generation of staff. Studies tell us that this generation values the quality of work far more than the size of the paycheque. Also, they are not hesitant to change jobs to grow their experience and careers. Therefore, leadership development and succession planning become very important retention tools.

The loss of key leaders and high-potential talent can be catastrophic if there is no succession plan in place. The stakes are high. The loss of a key leader for whom there is no back-up candidate can stall an organization in its tracks, causing a loss of profits, precious time, energy, and momentum. Negative outcomes like these can have a ripple down effect to more and more areas of the organization.

Yet, while succession planning may be of central importance to an organization, it is not always uppermost in the minds of middle and senior management. That's because performance is most often defined in quantitative terms. An example might be a target to achieve more and more sales, usually in the short term, to meet quarterly deadlines. And since executive bonuses are typically tied to performance, it's likely to encourage short-term thinking. However, progressive organizations prevent this from happening by linking part of the executive rewards to how they manage succession planning for their division or department. As the saying goes, "What gets rewarded, gets done."

I made a similar recommendation in a meeting with senior executives of a broadcasting organization 15 years ago. My comment was met with a great deal of surprise, as, at the time, this approach was unheard of in traditional compensation programs. Eventually, the CEO of the organization agreed to support this revolutionary strategy. From then on, at least during my time there, 20 percent of the annual bonus for executive team members was based on their contribution to the succession planning component of their responsibilities. All of the executives were measured on how they developed and implemented key learning and development plans for high-potential individuals in their departments to support succession planning.

The strategy worked. Many of those high-potential individuals became the top executive leaders of the organization within a few years. Hopefully, they have continued their organization's policy of tying rewards to succession planning. After all, it is the value of the people in an organization — the return on human assets — that sets the organization apart from their competition.

Who leads the succession planning process?

Who leads the way on succession planning? Succession planning must involve at least the top two to three levels of management. When this responsibility is shared, great things happen. Specifically, the succession planning process should be led by a succession planning committee made up of the vice-presidents of each department, i.e., marketing, sales, operations, finance, and human resources. Each VP is accountable for his or her own department. These VPs must demonstrate their commitment to the process. They must make people, time, and financial resources available. They set the budget (including enough funds to hire outside expertise, if required), allot time, and choose who in the organization will spearhead the process. These decisions, and how they are communicated throughout the organization, will send a message of how seriously senior management takes the succession planning process. This group maintains ownership of the process, and directly or indirectly monitors individual development plans. Ultimately, this group is accountable for keeping the process in the spotlight.

Just as an organization must define its values, so also must the succession planning committee embrace the key values that will make the succession planning process effective. These values are trust, courage, and humility.

Trust ensures that the sharing of candid and accurate information is kept confidential as an employee's future potential is discussed, in order to set the candidate up for success in the position they are promoted into and not to unintentionally set them up for failure. Failure can be costly to both the individual and the organization.

Courage is especially necessary. For example, it is better for a member of the succession planning committee to share controversial information about a high-potential candidate in the early stages, prior to the organization spending several years of additional training and development dollars. Many of today's businesses are complex and fast moving. Therefore, it is critical for executives to be confident enough to be upfront and share key information around issues related to succession planning. They need to understand that by withholding important information, they could unintentionally set up a high-potential candidate for failure.

Finally, *humility* is a key value to the succession planning process. Humility means understanding that you can be wrong. Executives need to ensure that their own egos do not get in the way. In the succession planning context, there are often challenges around the openness of committee members to share their areas of concern for the promotion of their direct reports, and not to confuse their personal like and dislike of candidates with the task at hand. Remember, style does not predict performance, behaviour does.

Typically, the VP of human resources coordinates the succession planning process with senior management and assists line management in preparing non-technical development plans for individuals, where required. In addition, the CEO/President and VP of human resources provide support for the other VPs to ensure that their divisions and departments are buying into the process. Most organizations today hire an outside expert to provide third-party objectivity in customizing the process. Managers at all levels also need to conduct solid performance reviews of their staff. Each individual should have his or her own personal learning and development plan to be able to accelerate.

An external coach is often used to accelerate the development of high-potential candidates, managers, and executives to fast track key performers. I have often found that when I am hired as a coach for an executive, it demonstrates that the organization values them highly enough to invest significant time and money in their current and future development. Following the initial meeting, the response of the executive is one of exuberance, feeling privileged and grateful for an opportunity to work one-on-one with a seasoned executive coach. They become highly motivated to work with the coach to further develop the skills and competencies required to become part of the succession plan for the organization. Executive coaching can be a win-win for both the organization and the executive who is being coached.

What does succession planning look like?

Succession planning must never be a free floating process, unattached to the other foundational statements of the organization. Instead, it must be grounded in the organization's vision, mission, core values, and strategic business plan. The strategic business plan should include not only the current and future direction and overall objectives of the organization, but also a list and description of the key leadership positions to be filled as the organization progresses. For example, distinctions may be made between technical skills, such as information technology, and other knowledge skills and soft skills. This has implications for the type of managers hired and developed within the organization.

Further, the strategic business plan should also include a list of key leadership competencies. These are the attributes the organization is looking for when hiring new candidates, and the ones it is developing in its current managers. These are the competencies that people should have to help the organization reach its goals. Examples of competencies may include business development, customer relationships (internal and external), collaboration and knowledge sharing, managing change and transition, interpersonal skills, and presentation skills, for example.

In general, to begin the succession planning process, the succession planning committee needs to develop a model for assessing the organization's current staff, to take a snapshot of where the organization is today. Let's assume the succession planning group is confident that they have the high-potential managers who have the inherent skills and abilities to do the job. The next major challenge is to develop and train them to align their skill sets to the specific needs and growth of the organization. This includes both leadership and technical skills that build on their academic or training expertise, whether it is in information technology, finance, marketing, or sales. As the organization grows and moves forward, the set of skills and talent is then readily available to fill the positions required to keep the momentum to support a leading-edge organization. In other words, the actions of the succession planning process and the actions of developing managers, leaders, and executives need to be synchronized with the specific time-sensitive needs of the strategic business plan. When this happens, both the individuals and the organization can be set up for success!

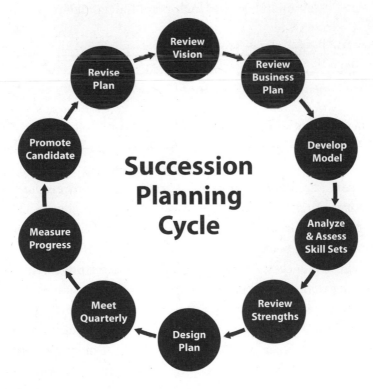

The specific steps in the succession planning cycle are listed and illustrated below.

1. Review organization's vision, mission, core values, and key leadership competencies
2. Review strategic business plan
3. Develop and customize a succession planning model for the organization
4. Analyze and assess the skill sets of team members
5. Review strengths and areas of development of high-potential candidates
6. Design individual learning and development plans
7. Meet quarterly — but include half-hour segments of succession-planning updates in other monthly executive meetings
8. Measure progress of high-potential candidates bi-monthly
9. Promote high-potential candidates
10. Revise and update short- and long-term succession plan for the organization.

My consulting work helps move executives and organizations through this succession planning cycle. How does an organization ensure a highly effective succession planning process and what is critical to making the process fluent? Research and experience have taught me that a highly effective succession planning process needs four key qualities: priority, commitment, continuity, and flexibility.

Firstly, succession planning must be a *priority* for senior management. As mentioned, this type of planning is often delayed because of the day-to-day and quarter-to-quarter pressures of the business. It takes strong leadership and discipline to keep this planning exercise front and centre at all times. The process of ongoing growth is essential to developing the just-in-time talent bank. Secondly, succession planning needs *commitment* so that the succession planning committee consistently follows through and implements the action plans. Those involved in succession planning must agree to meet regularly, and, between meetings, to be thinking and planning for those meetings. Thirdly, *continuity* ensures a smooth transition from one guiding hand to the next. As in a relay race, highly trained executives must pass on the baton to the next set of highly skilled leaders. And finally, *flexibility* is also key because corporations must adapt nimbly to the ever-changing needs of the business. This may be where the biggest challenge looms. It takes superb leadership to balance the need for continuity with the realities of change.

In the end, the succession planning process and the development of executive talent must be synchronized with the overall needs of the organization. The organization is then proactive and ready for the competition. It has the human assets to protect, enhance, and further grow the business. Organizations that do this excel.

The value add

Exceptional organizational leaders guide, influence, and persuade the staff on their teams to move toward achieving the organization's objectives, which are mapped out in the strategic business plan, and given momentum and continuity through succession planning. These organizational leaders are naturally motivated, with enthusiasm and passion, and have an attraction power that makes others want to work with and around them. When your organization and teams share a common direction and sense of community, the overall results are always greater than the individual doing the work. Utilizing the energy of one another makes it easier and faster to move forward as a whole. The following is a good analogy. Have you ever observed a flock of geese in the fall when they are heading south for winter? As each bird flaps its wings in the V-formation, it creates an up-lift for the bird behind. Flying in this formation means the whole flock can fly in a much greater range than if each bird flew on its own by utilizing the energy of one another.

Dr. Bob Eichinger, a consultant in leadership competencies who has co-authored several books and taught in prestigious programs on the subject, has developed a list of 67 competencies for leaders.[3] Ironically, he points out that the majority of leaders have skills that are virtually solely for individual achievement — integrity, intelligence, perseverance, technical skill, good boss relationships, and so forth. Fewer than one-third have developed people skills, such as how to coach and grow others, deal constructively with conflict, confront people and problems, even how to develop themselves personally.

And yet, organizational leadership is almost entirely about motivating, developing, and engaging *other people* to participate fully in organization strategies. In other words, the majority of people in leadership roles today are not well equipped to truly lead. This fascinating paradox explains much of the shortage of exceptional organizational leadership in today's business world. The answer lies in creating a climate of leadership development and coaching.

If there is a single business-culture standard that it would pay to introduce in every organization, it would be that every leader should coach in every interaction with others. The time commitment to do this has proven to pay off handsomely in saved time in the future, with dramatically improved business results. When leaders act as coaches to their staff, they help put them in the right jobs, and naturally foster an ongoing learning environment.

In my work with coaching executives, the skill-building exercises we do help them continually reinforce and enhance the skills they are using in leadership. What I have found, however, is that coaching is contagious. As a result, even if they didn't have great people skills to begin with, their increased self-awareness and understanding of how their behaviour impacts others means they tend to naturally develop and grow into a super coach themselves, coaching others to extraordinary success.

Sustainable and successful organizations understand how to continually re-invent themselves. Today's top talent are attracted to the most progressive organizations. These are the organizations whose leaders are able to feel respect and the work/life balance they value. But, far from just taking from the organization, these gifted and skilled leaders will make exceptional contributions to the organization that has a solid strategic business plan and clear performance management system.

With a solid organizational vision and highly effective organizational leadership lived out in the strategic business plan and the succession planning process, the organization is well positioned for the integration of organizational wellness. Highly successful executives, leaders, and staff working in a healthy workplace environment with minimum absenteeism and good work/life balance brings The All Together Now Advantage Model full circle. Organizational vision, organizational leadership, and organizational wellness provide the solid supports for the entire organization. When you have aligned your personal vision, leadership, and wellness with the organization's vision, leadership, and wellness, both you and your organization can soar like an eagle.

PART THREE

Wellness

CHAPTER FIVE

Personal Wellness and Physical-Health Management

THE MISSING PIECE

Most corporate executives I coach have a master's degree in business administration or a related discipline. Not only that, over the years, many have invested further time and energy in business education through advanced university degrees, workshops, and executive development programs, for example. However, though vision and leadership are common terminology in business circles, only in recent years has health, wellness, and work/life balance made an appearance in business curricula.

For many of today's top executives, wellness is the missing piece. They may be highly successful in a monetary sense, making big salaries and living in luxurious homes. They may be respected leaders in their organizations, learning continuously about how to master their leadership skills. And yet, often because of their high-paced lifestyle, they may eat poorly and be out of shape. Furthermore, they may be living at such a high level of stress that they cannot truly enjoy the benefits of their position, and may even be compromising their long-term health.

Developing a personal and organizational vision helps clarify what is most important in life, but wellness sustains performance and sets a leader up for extraordinary success. My coaching experience has taught me that when people have a crystal-clear personal vision linked to an organizational vision they are highly committed to, have finely attuned leadership skills, and good work/life balance and self-care, they live an unbelievable life. Not only can they achieve what they desire, they can sustain it. It is the integration of vision, leadership, and wellness that provides The All Together Now Advantage. Achieving that integration is a journey, not a destination.

This chapter delves deeply into the area of personal wellness. Because personal wellness has been a long-neglected part of executive success, this section is lengthier than the previous sections on vision and leadership. Unlike some aspects of vision and leadership, personal wellness is not as much about skill development as about life skills, and changing habits and behaviour. Like nudging the rudder of a large ship, it is amazing how a small change can make a dramatic improvement in life's long-term course. Personal wellness is a choice, and it takes courage and commitment. It is the sixth leadership competency of mastering lifestyle management and overall wellness as a role model in the organization.

Let me say from the start that I am not a medical expert. However, I have done extensive study in areas such as work/life balance, stress management, and human anatomy and physiology. In my early career, in addition to my full-time role in management at a large consumer packaged goods corporation in Canada, I was a certified fitness instructor and voluntarily taught staff fitness classes at the lunch hour for seven years. Over the years, and in preparation for this book, I have also consulted with a multitude of health and wellness experts and practitioners, including medical doctors, a variety of medical specialists, naturopaths, homeopaths, pain management experts, massage therapists, fitness trainers, athletes, and nutritionists. Finally, over the past two and a half decades, I have worked with hundreds of executives, and witnessed their most critical challenges in finding wellness in their demanding roles. As a result, I am in a position to identify, consolidate, and summarize some of these key insights for you. There are hundreds of books on health and wellness on the market. My contribution is to sift through that content and pull out the information that is of greatest use to corporate executives and high-potential leaders. I know from my coaching experience that these insights can make a huge difference to the personal life, professional performance, and organizational success of a corporate executive.

THE WHAT AND WHY OF PERSONAL WELLNESS

How would you define personal wellness? Is it not being sick? Being fit? Not having pain? Being physically and mentally healthy?

Personal wellness has many possible definitions. I define it as maintaining a healthy mind and body that can consistently sustain the energy reserves you need to meet exceptional circumstances beyond your control, both in business and family life. As mentioned in the section on the key leadership competencies, specifically that of mastering lifestyle management and overall wellness, the ideal is to be able to sustain optimal performance by ensuring that you can get the time out you need for re-energizing when you need it, to avoid burnout from ever happening, because when it does, it's too late and the damage is done. For corporate executives, wellness relates to the lifestyle you design for yourself; a lifestyle that is reasonable, feasible, attainable, and lets you experience a high level of physical and mental well-being. Of course, some aspects of health are determined by our genetics. However, when an executive is committed to handling all aspects of his or her health and wellness that are not related to genetics, this can greatly contribute to achieving extraordinary success.

Our high level of exposure to books, newspapers, television, and the Internet means that we are overwhelmed by information about wellness with many controversial views — what's healthy and what's not, what we should eat and not eat, how we should exercise, and so on. But living it out in practice, particularly when leading the fast-paced life of a corporate executive, is a different matter. Sometimes the gap is information; more often it is a matter of self-discipline, and the right kind of support, tools, and coaching customized to the needs of the executive.

Remember that not living a life of wellness has serious costs. Every aspect of our lives are interconnected, and when we are not in balance in one sphere, it impacts everything else, including our physical and mental health. More and more research is pointing to the connection between things like the happiness of our relationships and the longevity of our lives, and the impact of stress on our biology. For example, Carley Sparks' book *Aging Smart: Strategies to Live Happier and Healthier Longer* says "Stress is not just something that wears us down and makes our muscles tighten up; it actually changes our *internal biological systems...* You can eat oat bran for breakfast and run five miles a day, but if you're stressed out, you're not getting the full benefits of eating right and exercising."[1] Years of over-stress in a career that does not use the skills you love to use can actually negatively impact the cells of the body and your long term health.

If you are an unhealthy corporate executive, it is not too late. There are things you can do to strengthen your wellness, physically and mentally, to proactively prevent disease, and manage your lifestyle from a whole person perspective. You can thereby enhance your performance, while reducing stress. By integrating your wellness with your vision and leadership, you open the gate to greater strength, energy, and vitality, along with more peace and contentment. And by aligning and integrating all three — vision, leadership, and wellness — you will be able to live the life of your dreams.

AREAS OF PERSONAL WELLNESS FOR
THE CORPORATE EXECUTIVE

Personal wellness and lifestyle management are critical to long-term personal and organizational success. Although wellness is a huge concept that encompasses many different issues and dimensions, in my experience, there are a handful of areas that are the greatest challenges for corporate executives. That's why I have intentionally selected some topics on wellness and not others.

The topics we will cover under personal wellness are highly integrated. Each of them is like a piece of a jigsaw puzzle. Alone, they cannot show the complete picture. But together, the pieces begin to make sense and come together as a whole. Some of the topics on wellness I will highlight relate more directly to physical health and well-being. Others relate more directly to our mental, emotional, and spiritual health and well-being. Still others relate to the practicalities of how we manage our busy lives. However, the fact of the matter is, they are all interconnected. For example, living a highly stressful life can compromise our physical health, and taking good care of our physical bodies can actually reduce our stress.

This, the first chapter of two chapters on wellness, focuses on the physical-health management dimension of personal wellness, and includes sections on skin health, dental health, overall physical health, fitness, and nutrition. The next chapter focuses on the lifestyle-management dimension of personal wellness, and includes sections on work/life balance, stress management, forgiveness, happiness, and personal finance management. Both chapters include important tips and tools that are specifically tailored for corporate executives. To close, we'll explore how to determine what works best for you in living a better balanced life to achieve overall wellness and whole person health.

PHYSICAL-HEALTH MANAGEMENT

To sustain your performance as a corporate executive, it is critical to maintain optimal health. I'd like to re-emphasize that I'm not a medical expert of any sort. Aside from having some knowledge related to anatomy, fitness, nutrition, etc., my role is gathering information to coach and support corporate executives from the perspective of their lifestyle management.

Most of the following information has been gathered over the years from highly respected physicians who practise Western medicine (science-evidence based medicine). Although many of them are family physicians, some are medical specialists and others work as medical directors for occupational health programs in large corporations. In addition, I have gathered input from some highly respected naturopaths and homeopaths. Although this information is up-to-date as of the publication of this book, keep in mind that all health and wellness related research is ongoing and changes with constant updates.

As the pace of life has intensified, one of the key aspects of lifestyle management is the executive's personal-health management. In an age where so much information is available, ignorance is no longer an excuse for lack of personal-health management. The objective for the executive is to be proactive in preventing disease by better managing his or her own health. Therefore, the wise executive focuses on self-care to avoid requiring health care down the road.

It has been said that the quality of most answers in life often relate to the quality of the questions. In relation to our personal medical issues and health management, it's of the utmost importance to ask the right questions. Without the knowledge to ask these questions, you are at a disadvantage when it comes to learning what you should know about your own health. In some cases, corporate executives may be intimidated to ask questions simply because they are not familiar with the medical or anatomical terminology. Clearly, articulating the questions is a further challenge.

Many years ago, after learning the anatomy of the body, I learned that I was able to communicate better with physicians, using their appropriate medical terminology. They naturally listened more actively, and were more proactive in providing an explanation of the detailed medical evaluation. Then our discussion could continue to a deeper level of understanding. Doing some initial research prior to visiting the physician can be a distinct advantage for you and the physician to maximize your valuable time together. On the one hand, you absolutely need the doctor's advice; on the other hand, you want to be in the driver's seat. After all, it's your body! And you only have one in this lifetime.

Under the broad umbrella of physical-health management, this chapter will now explore several important topics for the corporate executive, including skin health, dental health, overall physical health, and fitness and nutrition.

Your largest organ — your skin

Although we do not often think about it this way, our skin is our body's largest organ. In fact, the body's outer layer, the skin, can often indicate how healthy our body is on the inside.

Over the years, I have had a number of conversations with a variety of dermatologists about my coaching work with corporate executives. Dr. Stanley J. Wine (M.D., F.R.C.P.C), a top-notch dermatologist based in Toronto, Canada, told me that when his corporate-executive patients are under high stress, their minor skin problems become more severe. His recommendations for healthy skin and anti-aging fit well with the overall perspective of simplicity and moderation that I share throughout this book:

good nutrition, exercise, proper sleep, controlling your stress, and practising stress-management techniques, as required. He recommends a few practical and simple steps for maintaining skin health which are summarized below.

Firstly, use a non-irritating soap for cleansing and a good moisturizer. Executives should use what works best for them. In fact, he said that some famous and beautiful movie stars who stayed looking young for so long used the simplest routine — almost nothing. Although the condition of your skin is mostly genetic, it's important to clean the skin without drying it out. Secondly, the best anti-aging remedy is to be cautious with sun exposure, and to use a proper sunscreen. And thirdly, Dr. Wine also recommends that everyone have their doctor check any unusual spots on their skin or changes in moles at their annual physical. If appropriate, the doctor should refer them to a dermatologist.

For the purpose of this book, I will not venture into anti-aging topics such as derma fillers, skin tightening, botox, or cosmetic surgery. We have all heard about great results, and botched results. However, there may be a situation from a medical and individual perspective where some enhancement is required. If you do decide to pursue cosmetic surgery of some kind, do your research, get at least three opinions, and get several references from other patients prior to selecting a doctor.

The look of your face will not change who you are inside. In my experience, regardless of the external appearance of any executives I have coached, their outstanding achievements and personal happiness did not require facial enhancements. Dr. Wine very much believes that high self-esteem radiates natural beauty. I agree. Let me assure you that when corporate executives and other high-profile people, including broadcasting and entertainment personalities, have high self-esteem and inner confidence, it can be a distinct advantage, both personally and professionally.

Each of us is a beautiful human being, and valuing who we are, as we are, is what makes us unique and authentic. If you consider facial enhancements, you need to do it for the right reasons, with reasonable expectations about their impact.

Back to basics on dental health

The highly respected dentists I consulted with in preparation for this book all said that the main obstacle to proper dental hygiene for their corporate-executive patients relates to a fast-paced and stressful lifestyle. Faced with lengthy meetings, international travel across different time zones, and other irregular time constraints — believe it or not — executives often do not floss and brush their teeth as often as recommended. The dentists I consulted with shared that higher levels of plaque and tartar in the mouth can cause decay (cavities) and gingivitis (bleeding gums). An irreversible condition known as periodontal disease can also result, where bone loss and infected gums around the teeth can lead to tooth loss.

Keep in mind that throughout this book we view the body as a whole. The mouth, breath, gums, and tongue are often warning signs and strong indicators of the state of the body's overall health. Just like with managing energy and time, executives don't lack the information required for their dental hygiene. They simply need to make it a higher priority and take action.

Dentists recommend that you have an annual checkup and have your teeth cleaned every six months, every three or four months if you have a particular problem with plaque build-up.

Overall physical health

In general, good nutrition is the foundation to overall physical health including hormonal health. But how many male and female corporate executives truly understand much about hormone health? Not many. As a corporate executive, you need to be aware of what's most important to your short- and long-term hormone-related health. Why? Because hormones directly influence your quality of life and longevity. In fact, Christiane Northrup, M.D., author of *Women's Bodies, Women's Wisdom: Creating Physical and Emotional Health and Healing* says that, "Every thought you think and every emotion you feel changes your hormones."[2] That is why it is so critical to ensure issues related to hormonal health are included in your regular annual physical.

You also need to be aware of complementary aspects of hormone-related issues, because some physicians are much more knowledgeable than others on hormones. It can be helpful for you to work with a physician who is open to both Western medical solutions, as well as complementary (or alternative) solutions. Over time, you need the support and co-operation of your physician to make sure that if you need any type of medical services in the future, including any hospital visits, you and your physician can jointly make the best decisions for you.

From the perspective of complementary medicine, Janina Filipczuk, R.Ph., M.Sc., F.A.C.A., CFCP, CFCE, is an expert in bio-identical hormones and is also a compounding pharmacist. She defines compounding as the preparation of medication to meet the customized needs of the individual patient. She explains that an example of hormone-related medicine preparations are customized dosages in the form of transdermal creams, capsules, and so forth. She uses her expertise to work closely with physicians and other health-care providers, especially in the area of balancing hormones, which has greatly enhanced the quality of the lives of their patients.

Janina Filipczuk's expertise relates to hormones, fertility care, premenstrual syndrome (PMS), peri-menopause, menopause, and andrapause. These are extremely complex topics and each one could be a book in itself. Janina says, "The loss of hormones with age is inevitable. It is normal, i.e., an 18 year old man has much more testosterone than a 60 year old. However, you don't want this process to happen too quickly."[3]

For the purposes of this book, Janina has shared the following to make the information as simple as possible for the reader. She defines the following key areas:

- Fertility care is being in charge of understanding, maintaining, and evaluating your fertility potential, i.e., Am I fertile or infertile? What are the chances for me to conceive or have an infertility problem? In her view, those issues are best described by Gynecologist, Professor, Thomas W. Hilgers, M.D. (*www. naprotechnology.com*).

- PMS (premenstrual syndrome) is a grouping of unpleasant symptoms which a woman experiences more than three days prior to her period, i.e., painful breasts, anxiety, depression, fatigue, etc. PMS is a true medical condition, and the majority of the time it is hormone-related.

- Peri-menopause is the time leading into menopause and marks the onset of hormonal changes.

- Menopause is the cessation of menstruation in a woman. A woman is considered post-menopausal if she has not had her menstruation for 12 consecutive months. The average age of menopause starts at 51.5 years.

- Andrapause occurs when a man's hormones start to decline. Lower levels of testosterone make him less energetic, less productive, and less focused. In addition, this can also influence his mental and cardiac health. It's not uncommon for men to also experience erectile dysfunction (ED). When testosterone levels are too low, there's a potential to become andrapausal at an earlier age.

Asking yourself and your physician the right questions about health

To be proactive, it is important for corporate executives to have knowledge of the basics of their own hormone health. It is critical to be asking the right questions.

The following questions provided by Janina can be helpful in learning more about this topic. She has divided the questions into two areas: questions that male and female corporate executives need to "ask themselves" and questions they need to "ask their physician" in preparation for their annual physical. Some of these questions also include complementary options.

QUESTIONS FOR MEN

If you are **male in the age range of 30 to 45,** you should:

Ask yourself the following questions:
1. Am I becoming a couch potato and getting "love handles"?
2. Have I noticed a change in my stamina?
3. Have I noticed a decrease or absence of morning erections?
4. Has my sensitivity to taste decreased?
5. Have I noticed a decrease in my sex drive?

If you are **male in the age range of 46 to 60+,** you should:

Ask yourself the following questions:
1. Am I happy with my level of energy and strength?
2. Am I happy with my sex life?
3. Am I as tall as I used to be or am I losing some of my height?

4. Am I sad or grumpy lately?
5. Have I noticed a change in pressure when urinating?

If you are **male in the age range of 30 to 60+,** you should:

Ask your physician the following questions:
1. Does my homocysteine level indicate a "healthy heart?"
2. Do I need to change my diet to normalize my cholesterol, triglycerides, and sugar levels?
3. Do I qualify for testosterone replacement therapy?
4. Are you working with a reputable compounding pharmacist who can prepare bio-identical testosterone?
5. What is your waist-to-hip ratio?

For men, blood tests for Prostate Specific Antigen (PSA) are essential for the early diagnosis of prostate cancer. As a man ages, especially if there has been weight gain, he is prone to metabolize his testosterone to estrogen at an accelerated rate. Excessive estrogen can lead to prostate enlargement, and potentially, cancer. Men should also get into the practice of doing self-testicular exams.

QUESTIONS FOR WOMEN

If you are **female in the age range of 30 to 45,** you should:

Ask yourself the following questions:
1. Do I have regular periods?
2. Do I have pre- or post-menstrual brown (or black) bleeding or spotting?
3. Do I suffer from pre-menstrual syndrome (PMS)?
4. Am I prone to cold hands and feet?

5. Am I having problems achieving pregnancy (if desired)?

If you are **female in the age range of 46 to 60+,** you should:

Ask yourself the following questions:
1. When was my last period?
2. Has my sleeping pattern changed?
3. Do I experience hot flashes or night sweats?
4. Have I noticed vaginal dryness? Have I experienced painful intercourse?
5. Have I noticed a decrease in my sex drive?

If you are **female in the age range of 30 to 60+,** you should:

Ask your physician the following questions:
1. Are you open to complementary therapies?
2. Do you understand bio-identical hormones, or would you like to learn more about the topic?
3. Do you work with a reputable compounding pharmacist who can meet my unique needs?
4. Do you use saliva testing or blood testing to establish hormonal levels?
5. What kind of testing do you use to establish thyroid function?

Janina suggests that you should also discuss other tests such as the Pap test and breast examination (including self-breast examination) with your physician. If you are over 40 years of age, it is helpful to discuss having a mammogram/thermography examination. She emphasizes that there is continuous new research being done on these topics, so it's important to stay informed of new information.

Additional tests for both men and women

One other critical area to assess in the hormonal health of both women and men is the thyroid. Janina says that the thyroid gland is a master organ for regulating proper metabolism and energy. If the thyroid is underactive or overactive, hormonal health can suffer. Thyroid testing should include not only TSH and T4, but also free T3 and possibly reverse T3. If the thyroid is not functioning properly, it can impact the balance of hormones in the body. We now know that "about 27 million people have a thyroid imbalance, but less than half of them know it, because the symptoms — changes in energy, mood, weight — are similar to many other conditions."[4]

According to the medical information I gathered over the years, I was able to put together a summary of some additional interesting insights and key information that you may find helpful. They are as follows:

- A total and completely thorough annual physical for both men and women can include the following tests for health maintenance: blood sugar, complete blood count (CBC), vitamin B12, 25-hydroxy vitamin D, liver enzymes, renal function, lipid assessment, baseline electro-cardiogram, morning and night cortisol level (especially for those under chronic stress), bone density if over 40 years of age, urine sample, and test for occult blood in the stool.
- The homocysteine test is helpful for you to be proactive in health related to the heart. Ensure you ask your physician to check for any unusual skin changes, in moles, for example. After age 45 to 50, a colonoscopy should also be included for the prevention of colon cancer, and should be followed up as required, every 10 years (average risk) and every five years (higher risk).

- Along with the annual physical, a dental checkup and an eye exam should be completed once a year, or more often as required as a preventative measure. In particular, if you wear glasses or work long hours on the computer, this will ensure you have the proper lenses to avoid eye strain. If you have glaucoma, retina, or other related eye concerns, you may require a special eye medical exam, i.e., Heidelberg retinal tomography, etc.

In addition to the above tests, corporate executives need to make an effort to gradually learn more about key numbers to monitor your health. Keeping track of these numbers on an ongoing basis will help you stay proactive in managing your overall health. These key numbers relate to weight and body mass index (BMI) and percent body fat; blood pressure and resting heart rate; cholesterol (LDL and HDL, triglicerides); thyroid (TSH, T4, T3); thyroid antibodies; FSH; LH; cortisol profile; and DHEA (indicator of proper adrenal function).

It all starts with good nutrition as the foundation to your hormone health. Remember, your hormones directly influence your quality of life and longevity. That's why it is so critical to ensure issues related to hormonal health are included in your regular annual physical. Be sure to stay proactive and make any follow-up medical issues a priority.

Being proactive in understanding the fundamentals of hormones and your body helps provide you with key information to ask the right questions. It also ensures that by communicating your medical concerns with greater clarity, you will not only save yourself time and frustration, but you will also increase your chances of getting the optimal medical solutions when required.

Remember, it is your choice to eat healthy and stay fit. It takes courage and commitment to be proactive and become more self-sufficient in being an advocate of your own health.

Linking hormones and sex with personal wellness

Sex is an important dimension of our personal wellness, and relates to both our physical and mental health. An increasing amount of research is pointing to the fact that sex can have a number of positive health benefits, including lowering blood pressure, strengthening the immune system, improving blood flow, and reducing stress.

Despite the known health benefits, the busy, stressful, and fast-paced life of many corporate executives can sometimes make a healthy sex life a challenge. Hormone health can also have a strong impact on sexual health. Research notes that "An estimated 1 in 5 men currently experience erectile dysfunction. Although psychological reasons play strongly in cases in men 35 years of age and younger, physiological factors are the main cause for men 50 and up ... Problems in this area are linked to arterial disease, heart attacks, stroke and diabetes."[5]

In other words, erectile dysfunction is more common than we may think. Medications for erectile dysfunction are being consumed at an all-time high. Yet, erectile dysfunction is often closely linked to other health factors including obesity and stress. Some of these health factors can be addressed through better personal health and lifestyle management, including good nutrition and regular fitness.

In the end, trust and being relaxed with your partner is critical, because fear and anxiety are enemies of a good sex life. Sex with a committed partner promotes intimacy and a sense of belonging.

Fitness and nutrition

Personal fitness and nutrition are all about how you respect and take care of your body as you grow older. Your health is your true wealth. It is more important than ever for corporate executives to maintain their health. Corporate executives who experience the vitality of a life of personal wellness are able to reap the benefits of their hard work, right now, and right through retirement.

Fitness and nutrition are at the heart of personal wellness. It is no surprise that they are a $60 billion business in North America, and growing. Our knowledge of fitness and nutrition is evolving, with new developments and new strategies always arriving on the scene. What we know in 2011 may be different from what we know a decade from now. It's easy to become overwhelmed by the complexity of information. I coach my clients to focus on their fitness and nutrition from the perspective of the luxury of simplicity. Executives have ample challenges to sustain high performance in the work place. As a result, keeping it simple allows them to achieve their short- and long-term objectives, as well as to positively impact their longevity of life.

Fitness and nutrition are closely connected. There is a strong link between eating healthy and your physical and mental health. You will not be able to achieve the maximum benefit from exercise if you are not properly fuelling your body. Although there are certainly a number of general principles, the details of how to practice fitness and nutrition are unique for each executive. More importantly, the demanding lifestyles of most corporate executives can often create challenges for their weight. Some corporate executives are overweight with a strong desire to lose some weight. On the other hand, believe it or not, there are also corporate executives who are under-weight, and want to learn more about how to gain weight in a healthy way. When it comes to weight management, corpor-ate executives needs to learn what works best for them. Fit-ness exercises that work for some corporate executives won't work for others. Some prefer to swim, while others get their cardiovascular workout from running, biking, or hiking. Think about it. Even celebrities have major challenges achieving their fitness and weight goals, and they have access to some of the best and most expensive fitness trainers in the world. When it comes to fitness and nutrition, an individual's needs are unique. It doesn't matter how much you pay for the services, it's about getting it right for you.

Regular physical exercise has incredible benefits, not only for the body, but for the brain. For example, Dr. Joseph Mercola writes, "Exercise encourages your brain to work at optimum capacity by causing your nerve cells to multiply, strengthening their interconnections and protecting them from damage ... exercise provides protective effects to your brain through: the production of nerve-protecting compounds, greater blood flow to your brain, improved development and survival of neurons, decreased risk of heart and blood vessel diseases."[6] Some corporate executives have already developed a basic fitness regime that has worked well for them over the years. They maintain their preferred weight, are toned and in good shape mentally and physically and when they have their annual physical, the doctor is pleased with their overall health. Unfortunately, for most corporate executives, this is not the case.

The following insights have emerged from my years of coaching experience with corporate executives. Walking alongside them, in their worlds, has taught me that when it comes to fitness and nutrition, there are a set of common challenges that executives face because of the demands of their jobs. These insights have also been reinforced by my own experience in the past as a physical fitness instructor, as well as input from fitness and nutrition experts with whom I have worked, and who have a proven track record. I begin with the four secrets of achieving your fitness goals, and then provide some practical advice on selecting a personal fitness trainer and selecting fitness equipment for a home gym.

Four secrets of achieving optimum fitness goals

Over the years, I've worked closely with top fitness trainers who provide one-on-one fitness training for corporate executives.

In our experience, there are four major challenges around fitness for corporate executives: finding time and making fitness a priority, doing fitness exercises regularly, keeping a fitness program simple, and preparing your body in advance for any different kind of physical activity. The following section explores these challenges one by one.

The first secret to achieving your fitness goals is finding time and making it a priority. Finding time for physical fitness is much more of a challenge for a corporate executive than simply being motivated to get active. Many executives, both men and women, feel that since they already spend much time away from their families, taking extra time for self-care through fitness is selfish. However, it is far from being selfish — it is essential. To be there for others and your family, you first have to take care of yourself. More and more career men and women are beginning to understand this important principle of self-care. In fact, not practising self-care has significant costs. An old proverb says, "Those who do not find time for exercise will have to find time for illness."

For example, these fitness trainers tell me that some of their corporate-executive couple clients co-ordinate their family activities by having one parent take their children to hockey, baseball, or ballet while the other parent works out with a fitness trainer. They may switch and take turns on different evenings so both partners have time to work with the trainer. Sometimes both partners do their workout together with the trainer, once the foundations of their fitness program have been developed. However, current statistics indicate that, in general, career women still end up taking on more responsibility for the children and home than men. Partners need to work together and make fitness an ongoing priority and commitment to themselves.

The first step to achieving your fitness goals is to make a decision that fitness is a priority for you. Then, just like any important meeting, you need to include physical exercise in your schedule and make it happen. Initially, many corporate executives have a learning period as they realize that success with fitness and nutrition goals requires Choices, Courage, and Commitment to achieve. Adhering to their fitness and good nutrition over time can then become a lifelong habit.

In my view, some type of fitness program at the studio or home gym three times a week, or another type of physical activity such as walking, yoga, Pilates, tai chi and qi-gong (gentle exercise and movement arts that promote energy, balance, and calmness), martial arts, gardening, walking the dog, housework, raking, and physical work is a non-negotiable part of our lives if we want to achieve longevity. One important step is to determine what kind of fitness and exercise you most enjoy, what works best for you. For some, rushing to the gym to take a fitness or spinning class can take more time, and be more stressful, than doing an exercise routine at home. To participate in extra physical activity on the weekend with the whole family, keep it simple. Swimming, skipping rope, and jumping on a trampoline provide the fundamentals of a great overall workout. Hiking, tennis, and golf are also popular and fun family physical activities.

Although many corporate executives prefer to do their fitness program at home, they also need to find the time to do it while travelling for business. That's why they most often stay at hotels that have the basic fitness facilities (i.e. swimming pool, treadmill, stationary bike), so that no matter where they travel or vacation, they can keep up their fitness routine. Remember it's all about Choices, Courage, and Commitment to achieve your desired outcomes.

The second secret to achieving your fitness goals is to do your fitness exercises regularly and to balance cardiovascular exercise, strength and resistance training, and stretching. It is the consistency of regular exercise, at least three times a week, that helps improve your long-term health, as well as manage your weight. You also need to understand why you are doing certain exercises and ensure that you are doing them properly so that you don't get any injuries. Injuries cause set-backs and delay the results you want to achieve. They also can disrupt the natural rhythm of your body.

Whenever you can, provide variety in your fitness program to work different muscle groups. You can still do fitness regularly, even if you go away on the weekend or on vacation and there's no gym. If you are at a lake or ocean resort, take advantage of swimming and other sports, such as tennis, golf, walk on the sand, jog along the beach, hike, bike. You can also add variety by working out one day, swimming the next, dancing the next, hiking the next, and so on. If you are interested in sports, find the ones that come more naturally to you. When a particular sport fits your body type, it's more likely that you will continue the sport and have more fun doing it.

Health experts say that it is even more critical for women over 35 years old to focus on regular strength training exercises to prevent osteoporosis. Women in particular tend to lose muscle mass with age, and this can put added strain on the joints, hips, and knees. Many female corporate executives I have met over the years have learned this too late, and unfortunately their level of bone density had already decreased. You can be eating healthy, but your bones need more than good nutrition. This is also important for men, even though it is more prevalent for women.

The third secret to reaching your fitness goals is to keep your fitness program simple. The basics are aerobics, to exercise the heart and increase stamina; strength and resistence training to build up muscle mass; and stretching to keep your body flexible. To avoid injuries, it is critical that any weight-bearing exercises are performed carefully. Moving the joints and keeping your body flexible helps promote healthy tissue around the joints. This is also important to help prevent arthritis and joint inflammation as you age.

Do you want to keep it really simple? Dr. Roizen and Dr. Oz's book *You on a Diet: The Owner's Manual for Waist Management* reminds us that the only gym we need is our own body, and the knowledge of how to use it. We can use our own bodies for free, and design a regular workout that combines cardiovascular exercise, strength, and flexibility.[7] In their book, *Age Smart: Discovering the Fountain of Youth at Midlife and Beyond*, Jeffrey Rosensweig and Betty Liu give another example of simplicity for busy executives with great results: "If you just go out and walk 30 minutes, three times a week, and cover two miles during that time, you can reduce death by all causes by 58 percent and increase your life span by six years."[8]

Although some of the most successful corporate executives I coach work out on their own or with a personal fitness trainer, what is essential to their success is keeping the program simple. Surprisingly, great results can be achieved with a simple program and minimal equipment, which can include a small investment in a home gym, if that works best for you.

Alternatively, some executives work with a personal trainer for a period of time to find out more about their own personal fitness needs. Once they have a good idea of what works best for them, they continue much of the workout on their own while meeting from time to time with the trainer to change or revise their program.

Why do some corporate executives get better fitness results than others? The magic of achieving your best fitness results is a combination of doing physical activity or an exercise workout, eating healthy, and getting a good night's sleep to allow the body to heal, recover, and re-energize from the daily stresses.

By exercising and doing physical activity that you enjoy, you will naturally want to do more of it. These activities are small lifestyle changes that have a huge impact on being proactive to keep the body strong and healthy.

The fourth secret to achieving your fitness goals is to prepare your body in advance to play sports or do any physical fitness activity. Over the years, I've worked closely with many personal trainers who work with both corporate executives and athletes. It is critical for corporate executives to ensure they prevent injuries. Injuries cost them time and money, and lessen their quality of life. If you are going to play golf, tennis, hockey, basketball, volleyball, or curling, or get back to skiing or try heli-skiing, the wise corporate executive prepares his body in advance.

Some sports, such as golf, are often played by corporate executives for the purpose of building business relationships and creating business opportunities. In addition, some of these executives are invited to golf tournaments sponsored by associations, non-profit organizations, and charities. They often use these opportunities to network while supporting a great cause. From a fitness standpoint, you should prepare yourself and your body for engaging in any physical activity or new sport unless you regularly play it, or else you may risk injury. For example, if you are going to be learning golf or haven't played in a while, you probably haven't used that particular set of muscles for quite some time. To prevent injuries, you should exercise the muscle groups used in that particular sport and/ or physical activity or work with a trainer with expertise in human kinetics. These kinds of trainers focus on the disciplines of biomechanics and exercise physiology. They can help you understand more about your body's movements and how they will impact the set of muscles you will be using in a specific activity. In this way, you can more easily progress in the sport, more thoroughly enjoy yourself, and be less prone to injury.

This type of preparation is also important when corporate executives plan vacations that include a few weeks of demanding physical activity. These can include adventure trips, hiking, biking, sailing, skiing, and so on, anywhere in the world. Some corporate executives are so driven and competitive that they believe they are invincible. They think injuries only happen to others. But I have listened to stories of executives who did not properly prepare their muscles and bodies for these exhilarating, fun, and adventurous vacations. Many years later, they are still paying dearly with knee and hip injuries that, in some cases, have required replacement surgery. In addition, if they are overweight, they are also putting additional stress on their bones and muscles. As corporate executives move beyond 35 and 40 years of age, even if they have been highly committed to fitness all their lives, their bodies are not like they were in their 20s.

The wise corporate executive looks at the big picture and focuses on preparing for the physical activity of an exhilarating adventure, a golf tournament, or a new sports activity, while getting a good return on the investment. This means enjoying the sport or adventure, having fun, and relaxing while on vacation, and then returning refreshed and re-energized.

What to look for when hiring the right personal trainer

When it comes to working out, it is a distinct advantage to have a personal trainer who is highly knowledgeable about both fitness and nutrition. In this way, the trainer can set up a program for you that includes suggestions on healthy meal planning, as well as on-the-go meals and snacks. I have tremendous respect for fitness and health practitioners who can provide excellent advice related to the customized needs of an individual. They get it! They truly understand each body is different. It's not okay to submit yourself to the same set of exercises that everyone else does.

Having been a fitness trainer myself, I've met and worked with dozens of trainers and actively listened to coaching clients and colleagues about their good and bad experiences with them. Let me share some of these insights with you on what you should look for if and when hiring the right fitness trainer for you.

1. Where should you start? Ask your business network, friends, or relatives if they know a good personal trainer who specializes in the areas you require (i.e. core and strength training, kickboxing, preparing for a sport, etc.). When you have a short list, the next step is to interview them. As a successful corporate executive, you will already be highly skilled in the areas of interviewing and evaluating the results of their answers. Gathering this information will help you with your decision.

2. Always check the background experience and do your due diligence before hiring a personal trainer. This is an important decision for your own body and personal investment. The right fitness trainer for you can greatly enhance the quality of your life by providing the right advice and exercises for you. On the other hand, some personal trainers, depending on their education, knowledge, and experience — or lack thereof — can unintentionally cause injury to your body. It can then take weeks and months for you to recover. In addition, it's not easy starting over again with a new personal trainer. Do your homework and get it right from the beginning.

3. Ask your prospective personal trainer the right questions. What are their past experiences and

what results were achieved? Speak to a few of their current and past clients, as well as other health-care practitioners who have worked closely with them (i.e. massage therapists, doctors, etc.) to find out how cooperatively they work with other health practitioners. Are they a good listener? How do they keep themselves abreast of the field of fitness? Even if you are working with a personal trainer at a fitness club, be sure to check out the reputation of the fitness club and how they train their staff. What's the morale like? Do they treat their staff with respect? A positive environment for working out is important. Are the gym, equipment, and change rooms clean?

4. If you can, try to intuitively pick up how well the personal trainer knows their own body. If they don't have a good handle on understanding their own physiology, how can they do a great job of understanding yours? Is the trainer confident and assertive enough to be tough with you in a professional way when it's necessary? Know what you are looking for and ensure the trainer has the proper expertise for the area of fitness you require. Most personal trainers have a specialty area. If you want to strengthen your core, find a trainer who can develop a program for you that will focus on how you can best achieve results in that area. If you want to take up kickboxing, find a trainer who can best introduce you to the safe way to do these exercises. If you want to prepare to play a particular sport, or have a desire to take the sport you already play to a whole new level, make sure you find a top quality personal trainer or expert in human kinetics who can provide you with expertise in strength and conditioning training specifically for that sport.

5. Evaluate how intuitive the prospective trainer is about your body. Do they ask you the right questions to comprehend how your body works so they can customize a fitness program for you? Do they have the ability to see how proactive (or not) you're being at preventing injuries?

6. Do you trust the trainer? Are they passionate about their work and genuinely interested in helping you to achieve your results? In the initial stages, it is important to set the foundation for how and when you work together. Ensure you clearly communicate what the steps are if, for any reason, you experience an injury. This is important. If you injure yourself, your trainer will need to work closely with your doctor, massage therapist, or physiotherapist. They need to be a part of your health-care practitioner team, if required. You want to be sure that you are not put under additional stress when you have an injury. Personal trainers who are genuinely concerned about good results will respect the time off required to heal, as most top trainers want a long-term partnership with you. Any reputable personal fitness trainer understands this is your one and only body, and that integrity needs to come before profits.

Fitness equipment for your home gym: what will you need?

Have you ever purchased a piece of fitness equipment advertised on an infomercial late at night? Did you find out later that the equipment had too small of a range of motion required for the exercises you needed, or that the "one size fits all" piece of equipment caused you an injury? As a result, did you end up using it only a few times and it's now become a dust collector in the corner of your basement or garage? You're not the only one. Find out if it can be adjusted for you to use or get rid of it. Think about it. You can pay for many sessions with a trainer for what it costs to buy the wrong expensive equipment. It's not always necessary to purchase a home gym to achieve your desired fitness results. However, in some cases, according to your specific needs, a particular piece of equipment may be necessary.

Some corporate executives work out in private or public fitness facilities and some work out at home. For highly successful corporate executives, staying motivated is not about the latest fancy gadgets, equipment, or fitness fashion. It's about the results they achieve for their body. More machines and gadgets do not mean better results. What is important is that they do the right exercises for them, whether on their own or with a personal trainer. Each one of our bodies is different, and we all have different needs. In fact, from speaking with some pain-management specialists and fitness trainers, fitness-related injuries appear to be increasing. This is usually from doing the wrong exercises, performing the exercises wrongly, using the wrong equipment, or using the right equipment improperly.

Let's say that as a corporate executive, you decide that you want to make the transition from working with a trainer in a fitness centre to working at home to save time. For some, rushing to the gym is another stress when they can achieve the same results exercising at home. You would be surprised at the small amount of equipment many highly successful corporate executives use at home and still achieve excellent overall fitness results.

If you want to put together a highly effective personal gym at home, one that has the basic equipment that meets your specific needs, the best advice from the top fitness trainers

I've worked with is once again to "keep it simple." They suggest usually one or two pieces of equipment — whatever is best for you — such as a high quality treadmill or stationary bike. If possible, another healthy option is to walk outside in the park or on grass, which is a softer surface than pavement and easier on the joints. In addition, you can add some small apparatus such as a stability ball, a small bench, some free weights, some resistance bands, and a skipping rope. They also say that a high quality mini-trampoline can be helpful as it is an alternative to the treadmill or bike, is easy on the joints for an aerobic workout, and also good for the body's lymphatic system.

Where should you buy the equipment? The best way to avoid wasting time and money by purchasing the wrong equipment is to ask around. Ask other corporate executives in your network. Ask a professional trainer you trust who has the appropriate background and expertise to provide this kind of advice. A good trainer can help you find what equipment is best for your personal fitness needs, and can make sure that the price is competitive for the equipment you purchased. For a home gym, you do not need commercial gym equipment, which is used in fitness facilities that have large volumes of users.

Keep in mind that corporate executives are considered a major asset to their organization. As a result, it's important to avoid an injury. An injury to any key player is always a great loss to the team and the organization. Imagine how this could affect your personal and organizational objectives and, ultimately, the bottom line of the organization.

Many corporate executives continue to achieve their desired outcomes even after retirement. I've stayed in touch with many who have been retired for five to seven years, and they are in incredible shape for their age. They are very physically active and are excellent role models of physical fitness for their children and grandchildren. "Physical activity is the most powerful anti-aging pill ...[T]he most fascinating and important areas of research right now is the study of the mitigating impact of physical exercise on cognitive decline."[9] says Dr. Karim Khan, who specializes in sports medicine, falls, and aging at the University of British Columbia.

Remember, your health is your true wealth. As a corporate executive, you are responsible for your own nutrition and fitness. The magic of achieving your best fitness results is a combination of doing regular physical activity or an exercise workout, good nutrition, and the right amount of rest for the body to heal and recover from the daily stresses. By doing exercises and physical activity that you enjoy, you will naturally want to do more of it. These are ways to be proactive and keep the body strong and healthy. It is all about longevity of life and being able to live life with great vitality right through retirement.

Insights on sound nutrition

Most of us know that we should eat healthy. However, each of us has a unique physiology and has different nutritional needs. More than anything else, what you eat affects your health because foods have healing benefits that can help prevent disease and optimize your health. Hippocrates said, "Let your food be your medicine and let medicine be your food." Or as the saying in the small town where I was born went, "It is better to pay the grocer than the doctor."

When you practise proper nutrition, you are less likely to overeat. You'll also naturally start to make healthier food choices. The more you choose healthier foods, you will gradually become accustomed to and prefer their taste. In short, the more you eat healthy foods and continue to exercise, the healthier you will be. What it really comes down to is that you need to be accountable for what you eat. As the old saying goes,

"You are what you eat." However, you could also say, "You are what you digest." The healthier you are, the greater the ability for your body to absorb and digest the nutrients from the food you eat. Every choice you make with the food you eat matters, now and for your future health.

Nutrition is a complex topic, as well as an enormous field of constant scientific discoveries and new health products and information. In fact, modern food science is only getting to the tip of the iceberg when it comes to knowledge about the nutritional benefits that whole food can offer. Nutrition refers to the process of how the body assimilates the food you eat in order to grow and replace your body's tissues to sustain good health. What is important for the corporate executive is to keep abreast of the main areas that impact their health and lifestyle. My goal in this section is to keep it simple, and to focus on basic nutritional insights and information that are geared to the lifestyle of corporate executives.

We need to eat healthily. But we also want to have fun. A nice glass of red wine or a piece of high quality dark chocolate is healthy in reasonable amounts. If you are eating properly 80 percent of the time, you can allow yourself to eat special treats 20 percent of the time, according to the nutrition experts I consulted. Some of the corporate executives I've coached have achieved this ratio. In fact, many of them are now enjoying their new nutritional behaviour so much, that they have graduated to eating properly 90 percent of the time, and only venture away from the healthier foods about 10 percent of the time. If this sounds difficult, don't be too hard on yourself. Changes to our eating habits do not happen overnight. They are tiny steps that eventually make a big difference in your nutritional habits and knowledge of what works best for you.

Corporate executives face a set of common challenges related to nutrition because of the demands of their jobs.

Over the years, I have compiled information on nutrition from a wide variety of experts including nutritionists, medical doctors, naturopaths, and homeopaths. The nutrition experts I have been privileged to learn from have a proven track record, along with my trust and respect. In this section I have condensed these insights with an eye to the busy lives of corporate executives. I begin with the four secrets of achieving your optimum nutrition goals, and then provide some brief comments on vitamins, supplements, herbs, and antioxidants. The section closes with some practical advice on finding the right health practitioner (nutritionist, medical doctor, naturopath, or homeopath) who can provide you with a nutritional guideline or program to meet your specific needs, if required.

Four secrets of achieving optimum nutrition goals

Over the years, I have met with many nutrition experts who provide their services for customized nutritional programs to corporate executives. From them, I have learned that there are four major challenges around nutrition for corporate executives: what to eat, when to eat, how to eat, and how much to eat. The following section explores these challenges one by one. Meeting each of these challenges armed with good information and support is what will help you achieve your nutrition goals.

The first secret to achieving your optimum nutrition goals is knowing what to eat. Whether athletes or corporate executives, every human being needs the proper fuel to be healthy. Without it, they will not be very efficient or focused on performance. By properly fuelling their bodies, they can maximize their productivity and minimize stress.

To keep it simple, you want to eat plenty of fruits and vegetables and fibre (30 to 35 grams a day), particularly a variety of colourful fruits and vegetables in shades such as orange, red, purple, and yellow. Eating lots of salads with raw and lightly steamed colourful vegetables (lettuce, carrots, celery, cucumbers, olives, tomatoes, broccoli, spinach, peas, beans, peppers, cauliflower, onions, swiss chard, and kale) are good choices. It is also important to eat an adequate amount of fruits (apples, oranges, grapefruits, peaches, pears, bananas, pineapple, kiwi, mango, cherries, blackberries, blueberries, raspberries, strawberries, and watermelon). Nutrition experts say that the best way to continually cleanse the body naturally is through proper nutrition. The body naturally detoxifies itself that way.

When possible, eat fish, whole grains, and fresh vegetables and drink plenty of water to stay hydrated. You can replace meat and fish with legumes and beans (garbanzo, adzuki, navy, and black beans). Adding brown rice is also a healthy option and great for variety. Homemade soups are another idea for how to combine nutritious foods in one delicious meal. Herbs and spices such as ginger, rosemary, turmeric, curry, cumin, marjoram, basil, garlic, oregano, cilantro, dill, parsley, cinnamon, and so on add amazing flavour to your meals. Whenever time permits, make the best possible food choices that will nourish the body such as whole grains, unrefined and unprocessed foods, hummus, fruits, nuts, and seeds. These are classified as wholesome nutritious foods and can be used to create small meals. In a nutshell, you want to eat foods that keep your blood sugar balanced, and you want to avoid too much saturated fat.

A few more helpful tips for executives on the go: avoid buffets and resist second helpings. Whenever possible, try to have your food fresh and whole versus in cans, jars, and boxes that require more salt and sugar additives to preserve the food. When dining out, order a salad with the dressing on the side, a grilled or baked entree such as fish or chicken instead of a fried entree, and have steamed vegetables. For dessert, fresh fruit with cheese is a healthy choice.

There are a number of options available for the busy corporate executive in a fast-paced business world to incorporate healthy nutrition. Healthy smoothies or liquid nutrition can be made quickly or purchased. There are also nutritional health bars, and you can make your own trail-mix with raw seeds, nuts, and dried fruit. These choices often require being proactive to be sure you have a few of these on-the-go meal replacements, including protein bars and protein drinks, with you when you need them.

When eating out, choose the healthiest main course on the menu. If you are attending a big business dinner, recognize that some alcoholic beverages are healthier than others, such as red wine. For dessert, if you have a sweet craving, opt for fresh or dried fruit, or some exquisite dark chocolate.

Let me share a story about food cravings and chocolate with you. In the early nineties, I worked in the broadcasting industry. During that time, I went to a spa in the United States to take some time to re-energize. One of the speakers and educators there was Dr. Dean Ornish. I was privileged to have some time with him on my own, so shared with him that I was a chocoholic. I knew as I got older this would affect my weight, but I absolutely loved chocolates! What could I do to change that. I was happy to learn from Dr. Ornish that when I had a craving for chocolate, I did not need to deprive myself. His recommendation is to take a bite of some high quality dark chocolate and savour it and seduce it in your mouth for about 20 minutes. It works!

Trying new, healthier food choices allows you to avoid the negative and delight in the positive, each meal becoming a mini-adventure for your taste buds. It's amazing how, when you begin to eat more healthily, over time your flavour preferences change and you will no longer have any desire to eat some of the food you ate previously.

Like most anything else, when purchasing food, you get what you pay for. However, by eating higher quality foods, you can gather greater pleasure, and often eat less. One strategy to have a higher quality of food is to purchase local produce and fruits when available.

My experience coaching executives along with my research on nutrition has shown me how important fibre is to good nutrition and a healthy life. Brenda Watson, certified nutrition consultant and author of *The Fiber35 Diet* with Dr. Leonard Smith, writes:

> Today, if a scientist working in a laboratory discovered a "new" ingredient called fiber, it would be hailed as a miracle nutrient, and one of the greatest medical discoveries of all time.... Every major network would put the discoverer of fiber, and his miracle ingredient, on the nightly news; and 60 *Minutes* would do an in-depth report. A Nobel Prize would be awarded to the scientist who brought forth this medical miracle. Why? Because today, the most respected scientific research institutions in the world have proved that fiber is the "secret" ingredient that will help you lose weight, prevent disease, and achieve optimum health. Researchers have found evidence to prove that fiber increases satiety (the feeling of fullness), dampens hunger, and reduces caloric intake. And researchers agree that a high-fiber diet can help prevent most of the major diseases of today, from heart disease to diabetes to cancer.[10]

Watson shares that digestive health problems and issues are directly related to lack of adequate fibre and result from inflammation of the digestive tract. She recommends these sources of fibre: apples, cranberries, peaches, barley, lentils, peas, beets, oat bran, carrots, oranges, cauliflower, potato skins, whole grain cereals, dried beans, root-vegetable skins, whole grain oatmeal, flaxseed, sour plums, whole grain pasta, fruit skins, wheat bran, popcorn, and whole grain breads.

What is this miraculous substance called fibre? Fibre is "the part of food that cannot be digested or broken down into a form of energy for the body. That is why it has no calories. It is considered a type of complex carbohydrate, but it cannot be absorbed to produce energy. And it comes only from plants: fruits, vegetables, nuts, seeds, and grains. No animal products contain fiber.... Fiber is not technically a nutrient, since we cannot digest it. But while fiber itself contains no nutrients, the food in which it is found is loaded with them, and this is a powerful dietary connection. Where you find fiber, you find great healthy-giving nutrition."[11]

Little by little, by paying attention to the ingredients of the products we purchase, by making healthy choices about what we eat, by eating plenty of vegetables and fruits and the fibre they include, we learn more about what works best for us and what is most healthy to eat. Figuring out what to eat is the first step in achieving our optimum nutrition goals.

The second secret to achieving your nutrition goals is knowing when to eat. For corporate executives, the most important meal of all is breakfast. Breakfast means "break the fast." You have been sleeping all night and your body is waiting to be nourished after seven or eight hours of sleep.

The importance of self-awareness is one of the underlying themes of this book, and applies to eating as well. If you listen to your body, you will be more in tune with two important naturally produced hormones called leptin and ghrelin. Leptin sends a signal to your brain indicating hunger. That signal means you should have something to eat, if possible. Ghrelin sends a message to your brain indicating that you are full. When you are in sync with these messages, it can help prevent you from getting overly hungry or overeating. These hormones naturally tell you what the body needs at the right time.

Ideally, you want to incorporate five small meals throughout the day to keep your blood sugar and energy level in check. Research indicates that the body functions best when you eat at regular intervals. That is often a huge challenge for most executives. They have an extremely busy work schedule, attend many business functions, and often need to travel on business. If you are in that category, you are not alone. Eating three meals a day, with two small snacks — for example, an apple with a few almonds, yogurt with nuts or fruit, or a banana — is feasible for some. Whenever possible, it is important to make time to eat. When you are travelling internationally, it is important to listen to your body, and not to eat according to your regular meal times, but rather according to your needs and hunger. Finally, it is best to not eat meals too late in the day; eat your last meal preferably before 7:00 p.m. when possible, especially if you want to lose or maintain your weight.

The third secret to achieving your optimum nutrition goals is knowing how to eat. Many of us can identify with the experience of watching a great movie on TV, and discovering by the first commercial, we have already eaten most of the popcorn. This unexpected overeating doesn't usually occur because we were hungry; it was because we were not mindful of that we were actually eating.

Corporate executives are often under pressure. One of the temptations that highly stressed executives need to resist is eating comfort foods as a stress reliever. In some cases, corporate executives — both men and women — have shared with me that they gained or lost 10 to 20 pounds after a separation or divorce. In fact, some have actually said, "I feel like I ate my way through my divorce." Nutrition experts call this emotional eating. It can happen when we are worried, anxious, bored, or even when we are relaxed and happy.

In contrast to distracted or emotional eating is mindful eating. Mindful eating is eating with a purpose, and to thoroughly enjoy your food. Being mindful of how you eat is critical for your proper digestion, so chew, chew, and chew. Experts say that you should chew each mouthful at least 20 times. When you eat on the run — in the car, at your desk, while watching television, or when you are otherwise distracted — you pay the price. Rushed or hurried eating negatively impacts your digestive system. This is mainly because it is unlikely that your food is chewed enough for the saliva to do its job to break down the enzymes for your body to digest. Be sure to not only listen to your body, but to practise mindful eating.

Whenever you can, it is best to eat with friends or family and loved ones in a calm and relaxed atmosphere around a table. That environment is much more conducive to proper digestion and overall healthy eating. For the most part, human beings are hard-wired to be social, and eating together provides a feeling of belonging. When you are eating and communicating with others, you are more likely to eat slower and savour your food. You don't just eat for the sake of eating, and you are less likely to desire a second helping or to overeat. Instead of just fuelling your body, your eating has become a social experience, and it is also healthier for you.

If you have time on the weekend, make homemade meals. This compensates for the meals that you had to eat in restaurants and hotels away from home during the week, when you may have had fewer options. Dr. Maoshing Ni writes:

> Eat mindfully. Most people eat too quickly, putting an unnecessary burden on their digestive systems. Your frame of mind is of utmost importance at mealtime; relax and slowly chew your food for optimal digestion and assimilation…. Chewing is a major part of

digestion — remember, your stomach does not
have teeth. The digestive process, particularly
the digestion of starches, begins in the mouth,
where enzymes are produced to help break
down and absorb nutrients.... Chew each bite
of food twenty times and savor the flavor with
joy, repose and gratefulness.[12]

The final secret to achieving your optimum nutrition goals
is to know how much to eat. We are all unique, and differ
physiologically by size, weight, metabolism, activity level, and
lifestyle. As a result, the amount you eat and your caloric intake
will vary by individual. There is no one-size-fits-all answer to
caloric intake.

Most people eat more food than their bodies need
to be healthy. It is much better to eat less and avoid the
consequences of overeating. That is why portion size is so
critical. Be sure to use your fist size or a measuring cup to
measure portions. To make it easy, the following are some
specific examples of healthy portion sizes. A serving of meat
or fish should be about the size of the palm of your hand or a
deck of cards. A bowl of cereal or popcorn should be about
one cup. A serving of rice or pasta should be a half a cup.
Nuts should be a quarter of a cup. A glass of juice should be
about six ounces.

Corporate executives often have great skills of visualization.
Be creative and use the same skill for your nutrition practices.
Visualize yourself as a sculpture with your desired physique.
Link this image to your nutrition insights and food habits
for portion size. This approach has worked for many. Your
food choices will affect the type of lifestyle you will lead as
a corporate executive. Over time, the wise executive will
visualize portion size and naturally be able to ensure they are
eating within their caloric limit.

When possible, it is best to eat a large breakfast, medium-sized lunch, and small dinner. This makes it much easier on your digestive system. It's best to eat until you feel about 80 percent full. This allows the body to digest properly. Executives who eat this way know that if they overeat, they will feel lethargic and want to sleep because their body needs to take more energy to digest the excess food. Having a high level of self-awareness and tuning into your body is extremely important when it comes to how much to eat. If you are consistently overeating, you may need to ask yourself why, and if it is really due to hunger. You can then monitor your eating behaviour more carefully to learn more about when this overeating is happening and what activity or incidents surround it.

Healthy eating and mindfully listening to your body will increase your energy, vitality, and overall wellbeing.

What about vitamins, supplements, herbs, and antioxidants

If you are a corporate executive who is lacking balanced nutrition, and you're stressed and not always able to eat properly, you may be considering taking supplements. These can take the form of multi-vitamins, individual vitamins and minerals, antioxidants, green tea, and herbs. In most cases a nutritionist or health practitioner (medical doctor, naturopath, homeopath, etc.) can help you figure out which is best for you.

The experts I have worked with emphasize that supplements do not replace proper nutrition. In other words, you should not be relying solely on supplements to improve and maintain your health. Supplements should only fill a gap for a lack of certain nutrients that you do not consume in your daily diet. By making the correct whole food choices, you can make progress toward achieving improved health.

Finding the right health practitioner for your nutritional needs

If you require a health-care practitioner to help with your nutritional needs, there are a number of options of where to seek support and information. You may choose to work with health-care practitioners such as a nutritionist, medical doctor, naturopath, or homeopath. These services can help determine what kinds of foods are agreeable or not agreeable with your body, including food allergies or intolerances. Health-care practitioners can also provide customized nutritional guidelines and programs for you to achieve your optimum nutritional goals.

Some corporate executives work directly with a health-care practitioner on their own. Others may have a personal trainer who is knowledgeable about nutrition. When personal trainers do not have nutritional knowledge, corporate executives may work with another health-care practitioner and share their customized nutritional program and guideline with their personal trainer to work together and monitor progress, checking in from time to time with the health-care practitioner.

Just as you would identify the best personal trainer for your needs, you need to carefully research and check out your potential health-care practitioner. Word of mouth is always the best first step. The next step is to learn more about the health-care practitioner's background, education, and practical experience, and to check several references.

For example, depending on their education, a nutritionist may provide allergy testing. However, if they cannot provide that service, nutritionists often work closely with a medical doctor, naturopath, or homeopath who can arrange for that service. Together, these health-care practitioners can provide nutritional guidelines and a program for you.

In summary, what you eat, when you eat, how you eat, and how much you eat has a profound impact on your health. The more you make the changes that move you to healthier nutrition, the more you can prevent disease, and the better quality of lifestyle you will have. To provide the best self-care, the three Cs — Choice, Courage, and Commitment — are also useful. Making the right choices for yourself, and having the courage and commitment to stay on track for what works best for your body and digestive system puts you in the driver's seat to sustain optimum health in the short and long term. By practising proper nutrition, you will be investing in your personal health. This will pay great dividends in building a strong foundation for your one and only body, and will enhance your overall quality of life and longevity.

BEING PROACTIVE ABOUT PHYSICAL-HEALTH MANAGEMENT

Being proactive about your own physical-health management is an important part of your personal wellness. We need to continue to be educated about the various dimensions of our own personal health — including skin, dental, and overall physical health — and we need to be equipped with the right questions to ask our health-care practitioners. Maintaining good fitness and nutrition has some distinct challenges for corporate executives. However, with the right approach, commitment, and support, you can reach your fitness and nutrition goals

Gathering these insights has been an exciting journey. Considering what I have learned, and how it connects to the lifestyle of corporate executives, their families, and the organizations they work in, has definitely expanded my knowledge of how each health-care practitioner can significantly contribute to their areas of specific medical expertise. Based on what I have learned from health experts across many fields, I truly believe that integrative medicine (combining conventional and alternative medicine) is the best solution to deal with today's many challenging health issues. When all of these health-care practitioners support and educate each other, as well as their patients, it is definitely a win-win situation. You will become even more knowledgeable in participating in your own health care through nutritional and lifestyle changes, and have more control over you own health. You manage your stress better and help prevent disease by eating healthily in order to consistently heal the body of any stresses when possible.

Defining and articulating your personal vision, matching it with your organizational vision, and demonstrating a high caliber of personal and organizational leadership can bring you much success. However, it is the foundation of personal wellness that will sustain that success in the long term and ensure that you can experience the best of life both now and right through retirement. By being a role model as a corporate executive, you can provide a good example for your staff, team, organization, and family and friends.

CHAPTER SIX

Personal Wellness and Lifestyle Management

WELLNESS IS THE SUSTAINING FORCE
FOR EXECUTIVE SUCCESS

Personal wellness means maintaining a healthy mind and body that can consistently sustain the energy reserves you need to meet exceptional circumstances beyond your control in business and family life. If you are a corporate executive, you understand that these exceptional circumstances may arrive more often than you might like or expect! With a solid foundation of personal wellness, however, you can face these circumstances with strength and resilience. Personal wellness is the sustaining force for consistent executive success.

Certainly, physical-health management is a critical part of our personal wellness. The previous chapter summarized important insights on skin health, dental health, hormonal health, and fitness and nutrition. Each of these elements presents unique challenges for corporate executives.

Beyond physical-health management, there are a number of other dimensions of personal wellness that are fundamental for achieving and sustaining extraordinary success. This chapter combines these elements under the broad umbrella of lifestyle management. Being committed to raising your level of self-awareness is a crucial part of exceptional leadership. But, self-awareness is also a fundamental part of personal wellness. This chapter on lifestyle management takes "getting in tune with yourself" to a whole new level.

Lifestyle management includes a number of interconnected components. I have chosen to highlight six particular elements in this chapter, because these are the topics that have brought the most value to my clients.

We begin with work/life balance, from a personal wellness perspective. "Maximizing Performance while Achieving a Better Balance in Life!" is my executive coaching practice vision. In this section, I describe what work/life balance looks like for the corporate executive, and outline a number of things you can do to achieve a better balance in life.

The second section focuses on managing stress to achieve a healthier quality of life. I highlight aspects of stress management that have had the greatest impact on the corporate executives I have coached. In this way, you may recognize some new strategies that can help reduce your stress, including mindfulness and meditation, rest and relaxation.

The third short section addresses image consulting. I explain that your image is a key factor in aligning your vision, leadership, and wellness into one complete package. I also discuss how getting a handle on your personal image, often with the help of an image consultant, can help save you time and money, as well as reduce your stress.

The fourth section on happiness is tied to the deep sense of fulfillment and satisfaction that full-fledged personal wellness can bring. I explain what happiness means to most executives, and how it is closely connected to personal vision. I then outline four paths to happiness, practical steps any executive can take to help find that deep fulfillment.

The fifth section on forgiveness, is not a topic you will

find in most business books. However, my work with corporate executives has taught me that forgiveness is essential for executives to be free of the barriers that interfere with their wellbeing and success. I invite you to read on to discover why.

This chapter ends with a section on personal financial management. I draw attention to the reality that many corporate executives do not spend enough time monitoring and evaluating their personal finances, and provide some tools on choosing an appropriate financial advisor. Finally, I highlight the power that can come from the luxury of simplicity and knowing how your finances can enhance your lifestyle in a way that truly and uniquely matters to you.

WORK/LIFE BALANCE

One of the most central aspects of lifestyle management is work/life balance. Personal wellness and work/life balance are about both your relationship with others, and with yourself. For example, wellness includes living a life that has space for quality time with your family, making time to communicate with your partner or spouse and children. And it also includes taking time for yourself upon waking each morning to experience calmness, even if it means getting up a half-hour earlier to meditate, journal, or appreciate nature, such as in the tranquility of your backyard garden. It is so important to start your day by connecting with yourself first thing in the morning to feel grounded in your day (ask yourself, "How do I feel today?"). Self-care is about taking the time to have a healthy breakfast, and respecting your body's need to digest the food you eat, rather than rushing or taking something along to eat in the car on the way to work. And it's about having the space in your life to have extra time to relax, such as when going to your hairstylist or for a massage, manicure or pedicure, rather than rushing to and from appointments.

Lifestyle management and work/life balance also includes other dimensions like taking quality time to plan the little renovation at the cottage or purchasing that piece of art. It encompasses the special time for a significant other away from the kids, to maintain the love and intimacy that bonds and heals and rejuvenates our bodies. It's about taking that time to ensure the family eats together at least two or three days a week. Whether it is at home or at a restaurant, what is important is that the family spends that time together. Business travel often minimizes family time, so this needs to be made a priority. Lifestyle management means not only having time for family, but having time for yourself to prepare for family activities. This might mean having the proper time to prepare a meal without rushing, or to enjoy purchasing a gift for a birthday party instead of racing through the mall at the last minute. If executives don't spend time nurturing the family during the hard years of work, they will hardly know their families when retirement arrives. They will have missed the best parts of their children growing up. Work/life balance means ensuring that you get at least one day of the week away from work to be together as a family to have fun. After all, that's the whole purpose of having a family — to enjoy being a close part of each other's lives and to be there for each other.

Are there important things that you've always wanted to tell your best friends, family members, or parents and never took the time to communicate? Do you arrange special time with your partner and children at least six hours a week for quality time, or do you all sit in front of a TV and pretend to connect and communicate even though there is no eye contact or two-way communication? These are all things that need to be managed as part of work/life balance.

It is critical for corporate executives to stay connected to their partner or spouse by talking things out on a regular basis. What is important to your partner? What is important to you?

How can those desires best be met? What is most meaningful for both of you to share? That is also why it is so key to learn the importance of having that balance, so that you achieve your desired outcomes at work and yet are able to reap the gratification of family and friends, the joyous part of life, a happy social life, and, of course, some time for yourself.

My experience is that the most highly successful corporate executives I have worked with are not workaholics. They are magnetically drawn to the job they love, and the balance in their lives only helps them be more creative and successful. When a corporate executive is a workaholic, most often there is an underlying fear that they might not have continued success. Or they may be avoiding family or a problem marriage, staying late at the office as a way to avoid dealing with the inevitable. On the one hand, some executives want to maximize their bonus to provide the most they can financially for their families. On the other hand, they miss out on many family experiences that can be meaningful and gratifying simply because they are not there. Busy corporate executives are often pulled in many different directions; one obligation competing for time against another. That's why it is important to establish healthy boundaries with both your personal and professional life.

People who have a good sense of balance in their lives take proper time to handle affairs of great value and importance. These might include doing research on a health-related issue to be prepared to see a doctor, reviewing banking and investment statements without having to rush or let several months pass by without paying attention to them, speaking with their child's teacher about how they can support the child with school challenges, or planning a vacation or trip for the family. Work/life balance means taking at least one day of the week entirely away from the office, period. A day for rest, some relaxation, time to take the dog for a longer walk, to do fun things like play golf or tennis, putter in the garden, or do tasks around the house — tasks that take minimum mental and physical energy.

In today's hurried world, we often neglect to savour the simple pleasures of life. For example, nothing matches the satisfaction of sharing a leisurely, healthy meal with family and loved ones. Carley Sparks writes, "Frankly speaking, the secrets to a loving and healthy life boil down to very simple things: eat right, get consistent aerobic exercise, get plenty of rest, be happy, have a purpose, and keep everything in moderation."[1] Doesn't this sound like what grandma and grandpa did, except their aerobic exercise was replaced by work on the farm or at home taking care of large gardens, along with taking care of the children? What's old is new again, it's just a different way to do it. And most importantly we need to do it with passion!

Some of the most highly successful executives I have worked with are people with a sound religious faith of some sort. Whether it is finding their purpose, or if their house of worship is a church, synagogue, or mosque, they greatly appreciate the faith that was instilled in them in their early years — or that they have come to later in life. In fact, this is often what helps ground them in facing some of the biggest challenges in their lives and work. While spirituality is part of religion, people do not have to be religious to be spiritual.

Many of the executives I coach mention how grateful they are that their parents demonstrated the importance of a spiritual connection to their faith. They shared with me that time with family and practising their faith, which often includes weekly attendance of an hour or two of worship, is something that helps balance their life and provide reflection in today's fast-paced world.

They know and understand how critical it is to ensure their own children are provided with this gift of enhanced awareness of their spiritual life for now and in the future, regardless of their faith or beliefs. You probably know from your own experience, that some corporate executives demonstrate a constant unrest and a major lack of contentment. Often they are not even aware of how they are projecting themselves. Having quality time with family — both for play, resting, reflection, and spiritual life — provides a value-add for the busy family today.

Often when corporate executives really take the time to discover and articulate their true purpose and passion in life — why they are here on this planet and how they can make a difference — it becomes their first step to consider their legacy. It is beginning with the end in mind, which creates a work/life balance.

MANAGING STRESS FOR A BETTER QUALITY OF LIFE

Lifestyle management and stress are closely connected. To say it simply, the more we master lifestyle management, the less we will be negatively affected by stress. Senior-level corporate executives will always have stress in their lives. It's a byproduct of working in a demanding, fast-paced, competitive environment while also trying to have a quality personal life. However, corporate executives who master lifestyle management, and put a priority on personal wellness, will have a much greater resilience to respond to or reduce stress

Stress is the emotional response to any condition whenever the body experiences change. Whether it is bad stress (frustration, worry) or good stress (encouraging, invigorating), it is still stress, and the body responds accordingly. Imagine that you take all your stress and put it through a strainer. You want the negative stress to fall through the holes of the strainer, while keeping the positive and exciting stress.

The way you manage that stress is what will eventually determine how stress impacts your body and your overall wellness.

The harsh reality is that a great majority of our illnesses are stress related. Dr. Dean Ornish has done over three decades of research demonstrating that comprehensive changes to lifestyle can begin to reverse even severe health problems without drugs or surgery. In a recent interview with Larry King, Dr. Ornish said:

> Stress does cause your arteries to constrict. It can cause the blockages to build up faster. It can cause your heart to beat irregularly. It can cause blood clots to form that can cause a heart attack. That's the bad news. But the stress is not simply what you do. More important is how you "react" to what you do. And if you practice some simple stress management techniques, you can be in the same job, same environment ... and not have it affect you. Your fuse gets longer as you can accomplish even more without getting so stressed and without ever getting sick in the process.[2]

Evidence from many studies and resources has proven that when we are under chronic stress, the aging process of the body is increased and our immune system is weakened. However, with an "attitude of gratitude," we maintain our vitality and can enjoy life more. In my coaching work, I focus on the positive wherever possible. When you handle difficult challenges or a crisis with a positive attitude, you have the resilience to better deal with the issue.

Perhaps you've heard the saying, "Don't worry yourself sick." Like many old sayings, it has a large grain of truth. Worrying affects the body physically and mentally. It keeps us from sleeping at night and wastes precious time — time that we can never get back again. About 90 percent of the time, what we worry about never happens; the other 10 percent, we don't have control over anyway, so what is the sense in worrying?

As a corporate executive, what exactly are the stresses you experience at work and at home? Very often, whatever makes you worry or unhappy is usually the trigger or clue to what is causing you negative stress.

Further, what are your stress signals? As a corporate executive sitting in your office or waiting for your next connection for a flight, from time to time, think about some of the following questions to be more in tune with yourself. What part of your body do you feel stress in? Is it your neck or upper back? Do you get headaches or migraines, sore legs, etc.? Do you have regular bowel movements? Do you have low back pain or pain in your jaw? Is there a tiny lump somewhere on your body that wasn't there before that is worrying you? Does something look different or out of the ordinary on your body, for example, a mole that concerns you? Have you had a dry cough for over three weeks and it's not going away? Have you been short of breath lately?

The bottom line is that you need to pay attention to these stress signals, and deal with the issues that are causing you negative stress in the early stages to prevent stress buildup in the long term. Often corporate executives are so busy that they procrastinate on the most important things, such as their health. You need to find out what the cause is, not just deal with the symptom over and over again. This may mean contacting a health-care professional. However, it is very important to make sure it is a health-care professional that you trust and feel comfortable enough with to speak openly. Have your questions ready and make sure you understand their answers. Any health-care professional who is an honourable expert in their field will agree that no question is ever too dumb to ask when it comes to your health, as your health is so important.

Remember that if you continue to ignore these stress signals, you will pay the consequences over time. As you work on your level of self-awareness and get more tuned in to yourself, I am totally confident that you will intuitively know exactly where your stress is coming from. Once again, you have the choice: ignore it, worry about it, or do something about it. The wise executive takes action right away rather than paying dearly for the consequences later by ignoring these signals.

For many people, their attempt to please everyone is a big stressor. We feel the most calm when we are in control. When we are overcommitted, we feel overwhelmed and out of control, and therefore stressed. There is power in the word *no*, and we should relearn it and use it. When you are able to acknowledge your limitation and your need for peace by saying no to additional burdens, you reclaim control of your life and reduce stress. Remember how powerful you were when you were two years old and sometimes you just said, "No!"

When corporate executives handle any interpersonal skill challenges in the early stages, they are naturally being proactive in avoiding much stress in their lives. Good communication and active listening skills plays an important part in stress-reduction. That being said, my experience has been that when my executive coaching clients practise much of what I recommend in this book related to managing life's problems and stress issues, what's left over is manageable. You will be as prepared as possible to have a reserve of resilience to better handle the issues over which we have little or no control, such as big crises like the death of a loved one, separation or divorce, a major sickness of a child, and so on. These are not things we can ever be totally prepared for. However, with a reserve of resilience, we can be better equipped to cope. We will then experience only moderate or manageable stress, instead of becoming overstressed or burned out.

As a busy corporate executive, your role will always be a challenge. While it may seem that there is little you can do about your stress level, by aligning vision, leadership, and wellness, much of your stress can dissipate. You will naturally feel more in control of your life, be more positive and excited about your life, and take the time to re-energize with whatever relaxation techniques work best for you. The ultimate goal is a better balance and living every moment of life. The first step is getting in tune with yourself.

Let me highlight two major groups of strategies for corporate executives to manage stress: the M&Ms and the R&Rs. The first group, the M&Ms, refer to mindfulness and meditation. The second group, the R&Rs, refer to rest and relaxation. Both groups are important strategies to not only manage stress, but live a healthy quality life.

M&M strategy number one — mindfulness

The first of the M&M strategies for reducing stress is mindfulness. Mindfulness is a specific skill that helps get you keenly focused on the present moment. It naturally allows you to be calmer and not get distracted by worrying about other things at the same time. Mindfulness is about "living your life as if it really mattered," says Dr. Jon Kabat-Zinn, founder of the Stress Reduction Clinic at the University of Massachusetts Medical School and author of a number of books on mindfulness. He continues, "If you're not mentally present in the small moments, you could be missing half your life."[3]

In practice, what this means is that whether you are reading to a child, feeding your dog, jogging, folding the laundry, or doing any other small task, you can be mindful of what you are doing and enjoy the simple ritual. Mindfulness prevents you from worrying, and allows you to fully take in the activity you are doing.

Appreciating precious moments is truly being mindful and living in the present. Whether it is a fresh spring rain, a waterfall, a sunrise, a sunset, or crashing waves by the ocean, we are all connected and inspired by the miraculous sights and sounds of nature. In fact, you can purchase CDs with sound acoustics of the waves crashing at sea — the adult lullaby to relax your mind. When you take a shower, do you take the time to feel the soothing warm water, the smooth soap suds, and scent of the shampoo? You have a choice: you can fly through the motions, or get up earlier and enjoy those 10 to 15 minutes for your self-care. Sometimes it is the most simple and small things that lighten up your day and relieve some stress. For example, I recently received a photo by email of my niece's baby, Emma, born just four months ago. It was a photo of one of her first smiles. It was a precious moment, one of the great stress relievers to mindfully focus our attention to a loving thought.

Do you take time to look at the nature around you? Is there a bird feeder or bath in your back yard that excites you when you see the birds splash in the water or eat the birdseed? Do you ever take time to observe the beauty of a butterfly or the plants in your garden? Do you have the patience to be mindful in these small moments?

Years ago, I took my then two-year-old nephew Sam for a walk. As we walked, he came across a caterpillar on the sidewalk. He watched that caterpillar move very slowly for about 20 minutes. I could tell by Sam's big, beautiful eyes that he was so intrigued, amazed, and excited watching this tiny creature. A two-year old taught me an important lesson about patience that day. With a loved one, like this, patience is easy; you willingly take the time to be with that special person you care about so much. On my own, I would never have taken 20 minutes to look at a caterpillar. In fact, I probably would have run away from it! But as I slowed down and also started to watch, I could truly understand why Sam was so intrigued by this tiny creature.

Do you remember the last time you watched the sunset over the water, the brilliant shades of colour with formations of clouds, and brightness of light in the background? Sauble Beach, Ontario, Canada, is known for its amazingly beautiful sunsets. Over the years, during the summer holidays, a group of us meet nightly at the edge of Lake Huron to watch the sunset together. It is a special time, usually after a long day of activity, such as biking, sailing, swimming, happy hour, and some fun with the cottagers, locals, and visitors on vacation. I have noticed that some evenings some of us in the group prefer to chat and relax while watching the sun set; others are more focused on observing the serenity of the sun setting. These colours of nature are so brilliant, and it is that special moment when the sun sets ever so gently that one can experience a serenity and peacefulness beyond belief. It's all about being in tune with yourself and taking time to relax and do what feels best for you at the moment.

When I am coaching a corporate executive, I often get feedback from his or her boss by the second coaching session saying that they are already noticing some differences in the executive's behaviour. Initially, this feedback perplexed me, as by the second coaching session we are only starting to get into some of the key areas of focus for learning and development. However, I soon realized the boss is observing that the executive is naturally practising more mindfulness. Although I don't use the terms *stop*, *look*, and *listen*, in some ways that is exactly what they are doing. This new mindfulness is the first indication that they are taking a closer and more serious look at their self-awareness and how their behaviour impacts others. By practising mindfulness, they can better zero in on what is working best for them and be much more observant and present in the situation. When I first meet with a new executive, they often tell me they want to achieve better results on the job, while not having to work such long hours. However, if they do the same thing over and over, of course, they will get the same result. Once they understand that they can't make things happen while continuing to demonstrate the same behaviour as before, they soon realize they need to be more mindful and more aware of how they need to change to get different results.

An executive coach is a highly confidential third party, an objective sounding board to bounce ideas off. In some cases, with the fast pace they work at, executives have never stopped long enough to really think about things, to really be mindful and take the time to listen more carefully to the true reality of what is happening around them. Often, they get off track without even realizing it, and it's difficult for them to put their finger on what has changed. By practising mindfulness, their boss will notice they are taking more time to have better eye contact, to listening more actively, to not interrupt, and to ask for clarity so that they understand more clearly what the boss's expectations are. Amazingly, the boss can often recognize this change in behaviour within a few conversations, or a single staff meeting. Mindfulness is an early and important strategy for managing stress and living a better quality of life.

M&M strategy number two — meditation

The second of the M&M strategies is meditation. Whereas mindfulness is being present in the small moments, meditation is "the practice and process of paying attention and focusing your awareness. When you meditate, a number of desirable things begin to happen — slowly at first, and deepening over time: First, when you can focus your awareness, you gain more power.... Second, you enjoy your senses more fully ... Third, your mind quiets down and you may experience an inner sense of peace, joy, and well-being."[4]

Athletes use meditation regularly to achieve optimum levels of performance. Just as we exercise our body, we need to exercise our mind. Meditation is a way to do this while relaxing at the same time. In my work I've found that many of the peak performers also meditate regularly to stay calm and focused enough to endure their greatest challenges. Whether it is high-performing athletes or high-performing corporate executives, both groups often have comparable skills and abilities among them. It is the psychological aspect that separates good ones from the great ones. The ones who have that inner mental edge, and who can apply it when it's critical, are most often the champions. In the end, it's about peak performance for both groups, so if meditation is something that can work for you, it's worthwhile to consider.

Meditation has been practised for thousands of years, and there are many different meditation techniques. No one method of meditation applies to everyone. The positive impact of meditation on our health, such as blood pressure, muscle tension, and mental sharpness, has been well-documented. It is important for corporate executives to maintain steadiness of mind, peace, and a calm disposition as then they are likely to breathe more deeply, feel more energized, and have greater mental clarity. When we are born, we breathe naturally. Over the years, as we get older and experience more stress, our breathing tends to become more shallow. Any breathing and stretching exercises are also good for our posture, especially after sitting at our desks all day. Practices including yoga (stretching, flexibility), Pilates (building on the core strengths), tai chi and qi-gong (forms of martial arts performed with gentle and precise patterns of movement) help us to breathe more deeply.

When we meditate, it naturally causes our body to calm down. That physical and mental feeling of rushing starts to slowly dissolve and become a gentle hush. This is a challenge for corporate executives. This gentle hush seems to slowly change into a more flowing and peaceful feeling. Practising meditation over time will allow you to have even deeper experiences of peace filling your entire being. Savour these feelings of peace. Over time, you can learn to very quickly rejuvenate and re-energize your body by using meditation techniques when you need to relax or de-stress.

Silence and time for reflection gives our body and mind a chance to relax and rest. Remember, when the body is under stress, the brain functions at a lesser capacity. By contrast, when our mind and body relaxes, it is much more likely we will get inspired with better decision making and solutions for our challenges in life.

Meditation helps slow down the mind to focus on what matter most in your life. Practicing the M&Ms is a journey, and unlike the business world, you don't want to compete with anyone to achieve your balance or discover inner peace. This is often a challenge at first, because instead of being about competition, it's about relaxing and letting the mind float; letting go of your thoughts, finding a sense of peace and feeling rested and re-energized. Meditation is about simplicity and silence. By focusing on a simple word or phrase the individual is able to learn ways to get rid of the chatter and clutter in the mind and relax and re-energize the body.

I strongly believe that to be healthy and reasonably relaxed in today's fast business world, executives need to use mindfulness and meditation in their daily or weekly routine to de-stress and get re-energized. These techniques also help to develop your reserve of resilience to better support you in accelerating your leadership abilities. Some of the added benefits are increased clarity of mind and inner stillness, as well as the ability to get more focused and increase creativity.

The R&Rs — Rest and Relaxation

The second group of strategies to manage stress are the R&Rs: rest and relaxation. Despite their many challenges and stresses, some corporate executives seem to manage their stress more effectively than others. In fact, they project a calmness. Why is that so? One reason may be because they perform daily rituals to remove themselves from the fast pace of their work. These small rituals can often add meaning to the complexity in their lives.

For example, one of the rituals that has been helpful for me is listening each morning to a meditation CD for 20 minutes. Even after two years of listening to it, I am endlessly inspired and never tire of the words, the serenity of the soft background music, and the angelic voice. I look forward to that special time of peace and self-care daily. Like watching the sun rise, or closing the day at the beach with the view of a spectacular sunset, it eventually becomes a ritual. It's another example of our body experiencing that same rhythm as the ocean. It's so peaceful. Recently there has been more musicians and medical experts working together on the therapeutic impact of slow, soothing music and how healing it can be for patients, in particular for lowering blood pressure and relaxing muscle tension.

There are also mini-rituals that we can incorporate into our day, where we can take a few minutes to breathe deeply and relax. It can be as simple as walking across a parking lot when visiting a client and being mindful of the warm rays of the sun. It may be a brief walk around the block at lunch to capture a few moments to re-energize. This may not specifically be meditation, however, it can be silence and time for self without interaction — just being, not doing — being in the moment. You owe it to yourself.

What keeps you awake at night and what is the best way for you to relax? For many corporate executives, the same two or three issues from work jump into their minds over and over again when it is time to go to sleep. Aside from mindfulness and meditation, some executives prefer a technique called progressive relaxation. In progressive relaxation, you imagine each part of your body from head to toe, totally relaxing one part at a time until the whole body is relaxed.

Is there a room in your house that is conducive for relaxation? What are the surroundings like? An interior-decorator friend of mine understands how relaxing the beautiful pastel colours of nature can be for some people. When I shared with her that two robins hatched in a nest on the veranda, she asked me to save the pretty blue egg shells. When I took them to her shop, she blended her paint colours to make the exact natural colour of the blue eggs. She used that same colour for some decorative paint in one of my rooms and also ensured that the same blue was in the fabric of the couch I purchased for the same room. Every time I sit down in that room, surrounded by those colours, I feel very relaxed and calm. That worked for me. What about you? What relaxes you? Walking, listening to music and the sounds of nature are relaxing for many people. I also find sitting at the lakeside, watching a sunset or reading a book to be very relaxing. However, not all these activities are available during the work week. We also need to find what works best for a period of self-care and relaxation during the week.

When your shoulders and muscles are tight, have you considered getting a massage? The tightness means that the blood is probably not flowing fully through all the parts of the body. Over the years of playing competitive sports, for example, using the same muscle group can cause scar tissue to build up. In addition, as we get stressed, whether from the office, exercise, or sports, we build up lactic acid in our muscles. Having a massage-therapy treatment can help relieve this stress. What is important is to get rid of the stress we have and deal with it in the short term so it doesn't become chronic stress.

For corporate men and women, massage therapy and relaxing in a spa from time to time is not a luxury. It is an essential and effective health-care approach to sustain good health. In addition to relaxing the entire body, massage can be a preventative measure to avoid chronic stress, as well as boost your immune system. One spa I've gone to for over 10 years is owned by a woman who is highly respected and knowledgeable on the spa industry. The vision for her spa is, "A mind at peace — A body rested and free from pain. A renewed sense of well-being."[5] The owner and the staff are so highly committed to this vision and the high quality of services and serene ambiance and peacefulness, that this is exactly how I feel each and every time I have left the spa over the years. The owner is highly selective in choosing the best healthy herbal teas, natural fruit juices, soaps, shampoos, creams and lotions, soft kimonos, towels, and pillows. She makes sure that her clients are pampered in a non-toxic and clean environment, yet with the soft ambiance atmosphere to soothe the mind. Try to find a spa like this to visit a few times a month.

Top-notch pain-management specialists and massage therapists I've had the privilege to work closely with say that the physical stress suffered by most corporate executives is mainly stress in the head, neck, and shoulders, as well as the lower back, and in their hands due to the computer technology and gadgets. The other key issue is that they often get dehydrated. They go to play a game of squash, tennis, or golf and don't drink enough water. Within a short time, their muscles tighten or they get a cramp, stomach pain due to lack of digestion, and often a headache. Our body is made up of 90 percent water and we need to keep it hydrated.

Over the years, I have gone to over 30 massage therapists, including pain-management specialists and sports-massage therapists. Each one is distinctly different in their touch. They have all worked on my body to break down scar tissue (from squash, tennis, running, skiing), provided stimulating massage treatments prior to running a marathon or playing a final tennis match. They have also given me massages for the purpose of total body relaxation after a stressful week, or to relax prior to a vacation. Similar to other professionals, my experience is that some massage therapists are better than others, so do your due diligence. Once again, word of mouth is the best way to find a good massage therapist. Keep in mind that many of them specialize in a particular area (regular massage, sports massage, etc.), so ensure the service provider has the exact expertise you need. They also occasionally work in conjunction with medical doctors and physiotherapists.

In addition to a massage or spa experience, having a reflexologist apply pressure to the reflex areas on your hands and feet is another amazing relaxing experience, especially for executives who are very physically centered. These pressure points correspond to the different organs and nerves in the body and promote healing. Most executives have their hands on computers, cellphones, or BlackBerrys all day long. Some executives are on their feet more than others. There are about 17,000 nerves in your feet that connect to all your organs. One thing I know for sure is that when women complain about back pain and knee pain, and they are wearing high heels to work daily, it can easily cause them physical stress. Wearing any heels over two inches can cause back, knee, and joint problems over time. Our body was not built to be out of balance wearing a high heel. I suggest that if women do want to wear higher heeled shoes, that they are more selective; not only about when they wear them, but also about the type of shoes they buy, as modern science has made some good inroads into this area.

Finally, with a heavy workload, corporate executives can easily get sleep deprived. This is a critical concern, because a high-quality, good night's sleep is vital for your health. Sleep is the best way to heal the body of daily stresses and re-energize. Although mindfulness, meditation, and rest and relaxation are important, there is no substitute for sleep. Alcohol and caffeine too late in the day can negatively impact a good night's sleep. Lack of sleep or insomnia can cause headaches and be detrimental to your health. Some corporate executives even have sleep disorders such as sleep apnea. It is important to check with your doctor if this is a problem for you.

When we are deprived of sleep, we lack concentration and our response time is slowed down. In my view, this is important information to take note of, because over time, the sleep-deprived executive can be less effective in skills like sound decision making and creativity, which they need to be successful. A good night's sleep can also help with digestion and sustaining a healthy immune system, because the body needs a break to re-energize and heal. The best remedy is seven to eight hours of sleep each night. Have televisions, computers, and BlackBerrys off by 9:30 in the evening. Give yourself at least a half-hour to wind down prior to going to bed. Gadgets like iPhones, cellphones, and BlackBerrys are helpful devices. However, if not managed properly, they force us to live in a state of chronic stress.

In summary, there are many specific strategies and activities we can do in our lives to reduce stress, while improving the quality of our lives. Many of the executive men and women I have worked with have participated in a variety of classes such as yoga, Pilates, stretching, toning, and flexibility. We all learn and grow from every program we take and eventually find out more about what works best for us. Whether it is incorporating those calming daily rituals into your life, doing an exercise class, practising mindfulness in simple moments, or integrating regular meditation in your life, these regular practices of self-care can be life changing — one little step at a time. There's an old saying that laughter is the best medicine, and it still holds true. In fact, did you know that a deep belly laugh can actually be a boost to your immune system? Health experts say that when people laugh heartily and often, it is like internal jogging. Many of the older and wiser generation share the significance of laughter in living a healthy happy long life. Laughing triggers the "molecules of emotion" in our body, our "feel good" hormones.

Even though laughter provides the release of feel good hormones in the body, it is unfortunate that, unlike children who laugh so often, we often allow stress to take away our joy and don't laugh as much as we did when we were younger. In some ways, laughter is like a natural tranquilizer. Taking the time to watch a comedy or read a book that is so funny it makes you laugh out loud is another stress reliever. Never lose that "feel good" child-like laughter that is so healthy for the body. We often like being around people with a good sense of humour, and it's a good thing as it's both fun and healthy for us. Even a smile helps. Which retail clerk would you prefer to deal with at the store, the one with the smile or the one without?

I have highlighted the M&Ms and the R&Rs as the two groups of strategies with the greatest pay offs for corporate executives in terms of managing stress. When it comes to the M&Ms and the R&Rs, the secret is doing them regularly as part of your self-care and stress management. The two areas that have been most beneficial to my clients have been firstly, to set a time for 15 to 20 minutes during the day or evening that is just for themselves, a time to just be, not do. And secondly, to slow down the body and mind by breathing more deeply, as it is so easy to unintentionally breathe shallow when feeling more stress. You will find that by practising these strategies regularly, it will naturally make it easier for you to achieve a feeling of peace and contentment. You will be more relaxed and mindful, truly living and "being in touch" with each moment of your precious life.

IMAGE CONSULTING FOR THE CORPORATE EXECUTIVE — NOT A LUXURY

Being in tune with yourself, including how you present yourself to the outside world, is an important part of lifestyle management. In the early years of my executive coaching practice, some organizations requested both leadership and image consulting, leading me to work closely with image-consulting experts. I now believe that you cannot have one without the other. Your personal presentation needs to be in sync with the message you are conveying. Your image is a key factor in aligning your vision, leadership, and wellness into one complete package.

According to Albert Mehrabian, a UCLA psychologist, you have 10 seconds to make a lasting first impression. Dr. Mehrabian conducted experiments that revealed how people perceive each other. He found that first impressions are based on the following criteria: 55 percent is visual; 38 percent is from our voices; 7 percent is from what we say. Clearly our visual image is the most important. People size each other up at a glance.[6]

I have often recommended to my clients that they meet with an image consultant. Why? When corporate executives can demonstrate a high level of leadership skills, are impeccably dressed, and have good manners and etiquette, they clearly deliver their overall message with confidence and outstanding professionalism. On the other hand, if they are missing one of these key elements, it can be a distraction from the overall message they are delivering. In my view, it is important that they feel confident and comfortable, rather than uptight, in social situations. They need to be able to put their client at ease by being able to introduce themselves and others properly, and demonstrate appropriate manners when ordering dinner and wine, eating, and so on. Since there are many excellent books to easily access information on etiquette, for the purpose of this book I will focus more on the whole package related to the wardrobe.

Many people seem to think that using the services of an image consultant is a luxury. Let me assure you that, until you can confidently project your best professional image, these services are a necessity. Working with the right image consultant will definitely pay excellent dividends in the long term.

Have you ever had to rush out at the last minute to purchase a suit jacket or a dress for an important meeting or presentation? Did this add more stress to an already tight timeline? Are you buying clothes at a favourite friendly shop, yet you never seem to wear them because they don't fit your lifestyle? Why not change "dreading to shop" into "dressing for success."

Johana Schneider, Image Consultant and Fashion Stylist says, "To be confident and at ease, not only do you need to be comfortable in your own skin, you also need to be comfortable in the clothes you wear. Your clothes need to match your lifestyle, skin colour, body type and personality. In other words, your clothing and accessories need to be comfortable and authentic for you — they need to compliment you."[7] She confirms that when you instantly know what to wear and you feel good in it, stress is reduced, time is saved, and you are automatically planning for success.

Successful executives have a personal vision of themselves that includes a balance between looking good and feeling good. For example, they don't have time to fret over what tie or earrings to wear. They have learned how to dress appropriately for their own situation, and their wardrobe reflects this knowledge. In fact, having the right wardrobe is a foundational tool for success.

When choosing an image consultant, it is critical to find the right fit and chemistry; it will be well worth it to do your homework. Working with the right image consultant can help you feel more confident as you learn to dress in a way that brings out your best. Choosing items to wear for a business, formal evening, casual, or sporting events should no longer be stressful.

While wardrobe selection is less complicated for men than women, it is equally important for both. When you match your clothes and accessories to your lifestyle and body type, you enhance your confidence in your appearance. Surveys reveal that people wear 15 percent of their total wardrobe regularly, so it is important that this base is versatile and of excellent quality. Learning how to build upon this base will become a pleasure rather than a chore, and you'll have a wardrobe ready for all occasions.

The right image consultant can make a big difference in your daily life. Finding the right wardrobe will save you time and money while greatly reducing stress.

HAPPINESS, SUCCESS, AND FULFILLMENT

Over the past two and a half decades of working alongside hundreds of corporate executives, one thing I have learned is that some executives experience much more fulfillment and satisfaction than others. I believe I can best serve the reader by sharing the insights that have been of great value to my clients over the years. I want to highlight what has worked for them in terms of health and happiness. What I have experienced in my work with corporate executives echoes the teaching and insights not only of the sages, but also of the most current research on the link between happiness and physical and mental health. There are shelves of books and articles you could read about happiness. However, my goal in this section is to condense the essence of these important teachings, save you time reading many books on the topic, and provide insights on happiness that are specifically geared to the corporate executive.

For some executives, it seems that no matter how much they achieve or accomplish, or how much money they make, they often still do not have a sense of inner peace and contentment. Some executives tend to believe that if they reach a certain status or fame — marrying into status, living in a prestigious neighbourhood, or winning the lottery, for example — they will have happiness. They soon discover that acquiring things, including status, does not result in fulfillment and satisfaction. Instead, they still desire more — bigger diamonds, faster cars, larger houses.

I hope you have been privileged, as I have been, to know people who are wealthy, humble, and generous. You may also know some people who are so rich they have become overwhelmed by their own wealth. Some people have everything money can buy, yet they are miserable. They automatically assume that more is better and that more will make their life happier.

Do you have the external trappings of success yet don't have the internal fulfillment you deserve? How do we turn on that switch to be happy? How do we experience full-fledged personal wellness, including a deep sense of inner satisfaction and fulfillment? Let's find out.

Linking happiness for the corporate executive to personal vision

Let me keep this simple. Most of my corporate clients do not spend much of their time philosophizing about how to define the abstract concept of happiness. Instead, they'll say this: "I'm happy when what I am doing matches my vision and values and I'm healthy and have a good balance between work and private life. That's what happiness is about for me."

In other words, happiness for the corporate executive is when their personal vision and values are a great match with their organizational vision and values, and all this is lived out in a state of excellent personal health and work/life balance. Who can ask for more fulfillment and gratification? It is by developing and articulating personal vision and a set of core values that the foundation is set for the executive to cultivate their personal happiness. As a result, I always design my coaching program with the ultimate goal of helping executives focus on what matters most to them. It's all about their purpose in life and what they want their legacy to be one day. That's why creating a personal vision is so key. By doing so, executives get to define happiness on their own terms.

Right from the start with my executive clients, I stress the importance of having a high level of self-awareness and an understanding of how our behaviour impacts others. This is critical to exceptional leadership, and it is also important in maintaining our happiness. Do you know yourself well? What makes you happy? What things are you doing when you are the happiest? Who are you with when you feel the happiest? The magic is staying focused on what matters most in your life.

When a coach facilitates a process for the corporate executive to discover, develop, and articulate a personal vision, it is important to include this important ingredient, happiness. In my work, I often help clients reconnect with their true values and beliefs — the ones that were most important to them when they were growing up. Over the years, these fundamental values and beliefs are often blended, changed, or eroded by the corporate environments we work in. Somehow, many executives lose touch with their core values; they don't realize how critical these values are to their happiness, as well as their physical and mental health. It is a privilege for me to help corporate executives extract their own insights, wisdom, and hidden treasures through the coaching process. These treasures then get woven into the unique plan for their desired personal vision. Remember, you have the power over your own life. Other people or coaches never set limits for your life — you do.

I've facilitated the personal vision part of the coaching process long enough to learn that the more you can discover, articulate, and experience what happiness means to you, the greater your chances are to learn more about living your dream. By contrast, if the corporate executive has not yet developed or articulated a personal vision, it is likely that they haven't spent a great amount of time discovering what is important to them in achieving happiness. So often, happiness is connected to doing what you love to do. When that happens, work doesn't feel like work. It is a passion. Part of that passion is the happiness you feel while working. Building the solid foundation of a personal vision helps naturally engage the corporate executive in more easily linking their personal vision with the organizational vision later in the process. It also helps them sustain their journey toward happiness and success with less energy expended.

You have probably heard the saying, "Success is getting what you want; happiness is wanting what you get." Only about 10 percent of people in the world are working in a job that gives them a high level of satisfaction because they are doing something they are passionate about.

The most highly successful executives I have coached also understand the link between happiness and the "luxury of simplicity." They know how powerful simplicity can be, and how it can help them achieve their dreams. Firstly, most executives need to ensure they are being paid their value and worth, that they are receiving an industry-competitive compensation and benefit package. Following that, it is the joy of doing their work that appears to be the real reward for them. They love what they do. They feel good about the natural skills they are demonstrating to achieve results. It is as much about the journey of doing the job as it is about the achievements. As Albert Schweitzer once said, "Success is not the key to happiness. Happiness is the key to success. If you love what you are doing, you will be successful."

The health benefits of happiness

Being happy has major physical and mental health benefits. An increasing amount of research is revealing the power of the mind-body connection. We now know that both positive and negative emotion have physiological impact. For example, with happiness, our stress hormone levels decrease, which can help prevent depression. Other new research points to the connection between happiness and improved cardiac health and a stronger immune system. These connections make sense because, as Deepak Chopra highlights, "Whenever you think, you are actually practising brain chemistry. So when you are feeling happy, for example, that is not just simply an internal state of euphoria. It has biological consequences. Happiness causes the secretion in the brain of things like serotonin, dopamine, opiates and oxytocin that not only make you feel happy because these chemicals are antidepressants but they increase your self-esteem and confidence."[8]

Statistics indicate that, for the most part, when people are happy, healthy, fit, and toned, more blood flows to all parts of their bodies. They are less stressed, and do not overproduce cortisol, which negatively impacts health. Being happy, along with having high self-esteem and confidence, allows them to age more gracefully as they have a high level of self-acceptance.

In short, when it comes to both our physical and mental health, happiness and positive emotions matter.

Lonely at the top

If you are a CEO, is it lonely at the top? If so, you're not alone. I have worked closely with many CEOs who experience this feeling. This feeling can best be described as being in a position at the top of an organization, where there isn't necessarily anyone at your level to discuss highly confidential issues with.

Although some senior-level corporate executives may actually be doing the work they love to do, they can sometimes experience a feeling of emotional isolation. Why? It may be high risk to discuss certain business matters with some of their direct reports, colleagues, or board members due to confidentiality, political ramifications, and potential impact related to their own performance and the bottom line of the organization. Yes, senior-level executives have their family, some close friends, and colleagues. However, these are not the people who necessarily have the expertise or in-depth knowledge to be an excellent sounding board for the kinds of discussions they require. In addition, some of these people may not have the high trust level the executive requires to think out loud as they problem solve, or be able to provide the necessary guided communication.

This is where a confidential advisor and executive coach can play such an important role. Top-level executives need a coach who is authentic and trustworthy, and who provides coaching that is genuinely in their best interests. When I meet executives who are feeling lonely at the top, we often begin by making the important distinction between loneliness and solitude. Dr. Jeffrey Rossman, clinical psychologist and director of life management at Canyon Ranch in Massachusetts says it this way, "Solitude is a vibrant state of engagement with oneself in which you feel replenished. Loneliness, on the other hand, leaves you feeling empty and depleted."[9] Every CEO or senior management executive needs solitude. Imagine how much information passes over their desk in just one hour. Solitude is a wonderful special time for self. It is "down time," relaxation for the brain. Unfortunately, for most of us, it is a challenge to relax and calm the mind.

A coaching relationship is an opportunity for an executive to brainstorm out loud on highly confidential issues. I've been there, and played that role for them. It is the reason why I have some sensitive insights on this topic that I wish to share with you. These corporate executives need to know that others like them experience a similar feeling of loneliness. I have listened and listened, understanding the pain of emotional isolation at the top. After all, there are some things that can only be discussed with a highly trusted person. It always comes down to trust. Further, the coach needs to believe in you and want to support you in your quest for success and happiness. Along with a high level of confidentiality and trust, an excellent coach combines "the head and the heart" to ensure the services provided are always in the best interests for the executive.

Paths to happiness

The definition of happiness is different for everyone. But, even across a wide variety of people, the paths to achieve that happiness have similar steps. So, how do we get there? How do we find happiness?

Let me highlight four different paths that have served my corporate executive clients well, and that echo much of the research and writing about happiness. These are: celebrate and enjoy the present; treasure and cultivate a strong sense of self-worth; nurture your connections with family and friends; and support a cause larger than yourself.

1. Celebrate and enjoy the present

Happiness is about loving life and enjoying life right now — this is the first path. The French call it "joie de vivre"; it's the excitement of simply being alive and enjoying a full life with the spontaneity that you felt as a child.

Being genuinely happy is good for your health; it is precious. We know that "time flies when you are having fun," and fun is part of happiness. Ask yourself, am I experiencing times at work where the mental stimulation, discussions, results achieved, and camaraderie with colleagues make me feel like I'm in the flow and time flies by quickly? Am I experiencing special evenings with friends or families where four or five hours together provides a deep inner feeling of belonging to a family or group, a letting-go feeling? This is an awesome experience. Some people experience this same feeling when their mind wanders off to the deep escape of reading an exciting novel, or when putting a complex jigsaw puzzle together.

Since being genuinely happy is precious, the biggest lesson for all of us is not to take happiness for granted. Have you ever wondered how your life would change if you had a terminal illness? How would it affect the "precious factor" of how you treat others and connect with them? Would you be more patient and understanding? Would you follow up when you say you will? When someone leaves you a message, would you not erase the phone message so quickly, but take the time to actively listen? Would you take time to open a door for an elderly person in a grocery store or office building? Would you hug a partner, child, or grandchild just a little tighter and with a bit more emotion?

Remember this "precious factor." You don't need to wait for a birthday or other celebration to show others you care. Our time is an irreplaceable commodity. We can't get more of it, so we need to value each moment of it.

Many executives tend to focus on the past and the future. However, it is living in the present that counts. The present is all we really have. The past is gone, and we never know the future. Successful executives love life and appreciate the little things that can add to their daily happiness. These can be as simple as time spent with a special friend, a walk on a sunny day, reading a good book, puttering in their flower garden — whatever makes them feel happy.

An attitude of gratitude in everyday, present moments is tremendously important — thinking positively and anticipating or looking for the positive. Having a great attitude has a ripple effect on the folks around you. A positive attitude is contagious. It naturally engages and empowers others, and enhances productivity. Author and journalist Melody Beattie writes, "Gratitude unlocks the fullness of life. It turns what we have into enough, and more ... Gratitude makes sense of our past, brings peace for today, and creates a vision for tomorrow."[10] Life is short. We need to live in the present, and be happy in the moment.

2. Treasure and cultivate a strong sense of self-worth

A second path to happiness is to treasure and cultivate a strong sense of self-esteem and self-worth; this is fundamental to happiness. With healthy self-esteem, it is so much easier to love life and have that desire to achieve our goals and contribute to society as a whole. We can then make wiser choices with work, friends, and loved ones, and provide strong support to each other.

Think about it, if you lost all your net worth in one day, how would you feel about your self-worth? If all your happiness depends on your executive position, your partner, spouse, or some other external person or thing, and if any of these situations change or disappear, you could be setting yourself up for failure. Years ago, I worked for an international career transition firm providing coaching and counselling to executives who were downsized. It was easy to assess how fast they would "land on their feet" and accelerate in their transition to a new job. The ones who were fired and had identified themselves solely with the organization with whom they worked for 20 years could not separate their identities from the organization. Sadly, they had emotionally become complete extensions of the organization they worked for. It was as though, when they lost their jobs, they also lost their identities. This is illogical: how can you be so valuable one day and not be valuable the next? Your value or self-worth should not decrease because you are downsized, or because you are getting a divorce, for example. If you allow your executive position, your partner or spouse to determine your self-worth, when things change, it stands to reason that changes in these situations can be debilitating.

When I coach executives, I sometimes need to remind them that you cannot love others if you do not love yourself first. I remind them that self-love is not the same as selfishness. In fact, when we nurture ourselves, we actually have more to give to our family, friends, and organization. I also remind them that there has to be a balance between giving and receiving. When we have a high level of self-awareness and are tuned into ourselves, we can recognize when there is no longer balance.

From the career perspective, many highly talented executives are being more proactive in guarding this link to happiness. These executives make it clear that they are providing an exchange with their employer. They will perform and get outstanding results for the organization; in return, they expect the organization to keep them marketable through leadership development and other technical aspects related to their career. Organizations know that a stint of three to five years often provides an excellent financial return on a high-performing corporate executive they hire. In fact, corporations often bring me in to coach these high performers once they have adapted to the new organization. This demonstrates their commitment to further develop the executives by tweaking and refining their performance. By investing in executive coaching, the organization gets an even greater return on investment within a short period of time. Most highly successful corporate executives I've coached have worked in more than one industry. This demonstrates their natural ability to broaden their scope and further prove that their leadership skills are solid. Truly, from a marketability perspective, regardless of the industry, it is all about the high quality of their strong leadership ability. And this adds to the executive's feeling of self-worth and happiness.

3. Nurture your connections with family and friends

Today's fast-paced world, with all its gadgets and social changes, has certainly fragmented much of what was once the old-fashioned family times, often centred around attending church, synagogue, mosque, or community gathering place. The message seems to be that these special times of deep connections in which families share their spiritual values are not happening as much as before. Yet, these times of family connection are key for teaching children more about values while they are young. With so many activities — sports, shopping, lessons — parents and children spend less time together. Many of us grew up spending time with our families around the dinner table. Meals were opportunities to communicate and share. Today, a regular family meal is so much rarer.

Dr. Dean Ornish, a clinical professor of medicine and author of the book *Love and Survival*, tells us that "medicine today focuses primarily on drugs and surgery, genes and germs, microbes and molecules. Yet love and intimacy are at the root of what makes us sick and what makes us well. Connections with other people affect not only the quality of our lives but also our survival."[11]

How would you spend your time if you had only two years to live? Why not start doing that now. When we stop to take a snapshot of how we are living, it is often easy to recognize that we are getting older and look back to wonder where all the time has gone. Are you spending time with the people that are important to you, the ones who enhance your quality of life and are meaningful to you? In other words, what really matters in your life?

How many people knew they would die in the 9/11 terrorist attacks, recent earthquakes, and tsunamis? These tragedies were wake-up calls to many people who take others for granted. Fortunately, for my clients and myself, staying in touch with the people in our lives who matter doesn't change after a disaster. We already know how precious these people are.

We know how important it is for the emotional development of children to spend face-to-face quality time with their parents and family. Quiet times together before bedtime, as well as evening meals together when possible and family activities, help the family members stay closely connected. Corporate executives who are parents can apply their active-listening and communication skills in a supportive way for their family.

As the saying goes, "Friends are quiet angels who bring us to our feet when our wings have trouble remembering how to fly." It is particularly important to decide which friendships you want to work on for sharing and satisfaction. Try not to take life too seriously! Follow your heart by spending time with the people who matter most to you. Be able to say "no" to stay on purpose for what's important in your life. We need to ensure that our life reflects what we most value.

Recently, I had a request to meet with a very high-profile CEO for a confidential coaching assignment. When we met, he said, "I would be willing to pay you anything if you could help me to not feel guilty when I take my son fishing on Saturday mornings during the summer." Often, executives will tell me that when they work overtime, they feel terribly guilty about not spending time with their family and children. On the other hand, when they spend time at home, they feel guilty that they are not at work excelling. It can feel like a Catch-22. However, since this CEO was already exceptionally highly skilled at leadership, once he discovered and articulated his personal vision and values, it became clear to him how he could have both an awesome family and work life, and live the life of his dreams.

Some of our friends are "forever friends"; some are not. This is where Choice, Courage, and Commitment are key. Do you have 125 "friends" on Facebook? It's important to know who your friends are, and who your acquaintances are. They may be contacts out there in cyberspace, but can they be there in person to comfort you and support you when you need it? What is important is to ensure we spend time and stay in close touch with the friends we do care about whenever that is possible. Nurturing these social connections is an important path to happiness.

4. Support a cause larger than yourself

We often think that achieving happiness will involve spending more energy and effort on ourselves. Self-care is fundamental to happiness, as is a healthy sense of confidence and self-worth. However, many thinkers and researchers on happiness increasingly appreciate that one of the important paths to happiness is to look beyond our own self to something bigger. Daniel Pink for example, writes, "Autonomous people working toward mastery perform at very high levels. But those who do so in the service of some greater objective can achieve even more. The most deeply motivated people — not to mention those who are most productive and satisfied — hitch their desires to a cause larger than themselves."[12] Eminent psychologist Martin Seligman, founder of the positive psychology movement, has also conducted research on happiness. One key to the meaningful life, says Seligman, is to use your strengths in the service of something larger than you.[13]

In my work with corporate executives, especially when we work on developing personal vision and values, we uncover what is most meaningful and most gratifying to that unique person. Often in the context of that discussion, the topic of philanthropy comes up — those efforts to improve the well being of all humankind and the environment, often by giving time, energy, or money to charitable organizations.

Although many of the executives I coach are on the board of directors of major charity organizations, many have not thought about philanthropy from their own personal perspective. Some tend to think philanthropy is for people in the calibre of Bill Gates or Warren Buffet. However, we do not have to have the same amount of wealth as Gates and Buffet to make a contribution and use our strengths to serve something larger than ourselves. One of my previous clients, for example, remembered the university scholarship he had received to complete his MBA, so he decided to give a small grant to the university, and include a substantial amount in his will for the same university. Another of my clients made a significant contribution to a hospital wing, after his mother had received such good treatment there when she was diagnosed with cancer. In the preparation of their wills, both the corporate executive and his mother included a substantial contribution to that same hospital. Others have participated in or given to international charities or other foundations.

What my clients have discovered is that being committed to and supporting a cause larger than themselves — especially one that has a personal connection for them — does more than just benefit the cause. It also gives them an immense amount of personal satisfaction and happiness. The contribution to a charity brings so much more meaning to their lives than another cottage or boat.

Tom Rath is a Gallup research leader who recently completed a study entitled "Wellbeing: The Five Essential Elements." Rath's research highlights that "An often forgotten element on many people's quest for happiness is philanthropy, which provides a far greater sense of happiness than exclusively seeking to fulfill our own needs…. Rath says the happiest person he met during his research for Wellbeing was a man in his 80s who spent significant time volunteering in his community. Although he had enjoyed a successful career, the man's main priorities and sources of satisfaction had always been contributing to his community."[14]

Many corporate executives have been blessed with so much. One of the paths to happiness is to give back.

Happiness as choice

There are many aspects of our lives that we do not control, things we do not choose. However, happiness is a choice. Robin Sharma writes, "Pleasure comes from something on the outside. Happiness comes from within. It's a state you create by choice. It's a decision. It's an act of will…. You can't control life on the outside. Hard stuff will happen. But you can control what goes on inside. And those who do become great."[15]

Abraham Lincoln said, "People are just about as happy as they make up their minds to be." It is human nature to strive for happiness; it is foundational and linked to our overall health and purpose in life. Some envy others who have it. Some of us think we will only achieve happiness when we are richer, thinner, married, divorced, win the lottery, and so on. We all probably know someone who appears to have everything, yet they still yearn for true happiness. In my view, true happiness comes from within and isn't based on our status, position, wealth, or possessions. It is available to all of us if we want to have it. In my view, from all the research I've done, it's apparent that happiness is a decision. It's a choice.

I believe part of happiness is making wise and well-thought-out choices about who you spend most of your time with, those who are supportive, for example. Time is energy, and we only have so much of it. It is precious and irreplaceable, so we need to value it. Some people are natural worriers. As mentioned earlier, they say that 90 percent of what we worry about never happens, and over the other 10 percent, we have no control. We need to let go. Worry can erode our happiness and slowly steal away our joy and time.

To keep it simple, when you have a high level of self-awareness, know what you love to do and who you want to spend most of your time with, it can greatly impact worry and happiness. Finding your passion needs to be captured and integrated into your personal vision.

You have probably had many different perceptions over the years of what happiness meant to you; it probably changed in your teens, in your 20s, in your 30s, 40s, and so on. What is most important is that the foundation of your happiness always relates back to a high level of self-awareness. That's because you need to "know thyself" well first, before you know what makes you happy.

The studies I have done on happiness, combined with the wisdom of the sages and my work over the years coaching corporate executives, has taught me that, although each person may define their personal vision differently, the paths to happiness are shared by many. Enjoy and celebrate the present. Treasure and cultivate a strong sense of self-worth. Nurture your connections with family and friends. Support a cause larger than yourself. And in the end, remember, happiness is a choice.

Free yourself through forgiveness — the most selfish thing you may ever do

Whatever the industry, we all know that how we are treated makes a difference. The way we are treated either motivates or demotivates us. My experience strongly indicates that corporate executives who demonstrate genuine humility with their staff are much more approachable and have a deep underlying confidence. Staff will share invaluable information and ideas with those who demonstrate humility, rather than with those corporate executives who appear to have big egos. What I have learned about coaching executives who achieve extraordinary success is that humility pays big dividends. And humility is fundamental to forgiveness.

Were you ever downsized or fired? Did you survive corporate downsizing because the organization required your specific skills, yet a few of your close colleagues were terminated? Are you suffering from survivor guilt? Were you ever denied a promotion or a bonus you felt you deserved? If so, are you still angry and feeling hurt and betrayed? How have these feelings affected your relationships with others and your personal health?

In a perfect world, there would be no need for forgiveness. However, nobody is perfect. We all make mistakes and we all have been hurt, offended, or betrayed at some point in our lives. Deep hurts can happen at work, or at home — often due to some injustice, unfair treatment, or lack of respect. On occasion, often without even realizing it, we can hurt the ones we love the most.

When mistakes and hurt happen, however, it's all about the "how" — how you handle the issues and how you treat and forgive others. Sometimes these hurts are easily forgiven, and sometimes they affect us so deeply that it can take a long time to heal. In fact, sometimes people carry their unresolved pain for years and years, like a wound that never heals. Taking the initiative for forgiveness in the early stages helps prevent the buildup of stress.

Did you know that as a corporate executive you can actually be living like a prisoner and not know it? I'm speaking here about your inner freedom. Many corporate executives operate in a prison of their own making. Yet, amazingly they often do not realize what a powerful tool forgiveness is to help free themselves and move on. Forgiving does not make the other person right and it does not mean you are condoning another person's behaviour. It just means that you have forgiven, let it go, and moved on.

If forgiving is difficult for you, that's okay: it is difficult for everyone. Try not to be too hard on yourself. For most people, forgiveness does not feel like a natural process and forgiveness tends to happen in small steps. Forgiveness is more easily said than done, because true forgiveness has to come from the heart, not just the lips.

Forgiveness may be hard, but not forgiving is harder in the long term. There can be huge personal costs by refusing to forgive. In many ways, we do not really have a choice. If we want to be healthy, we need to forgive. Why? Refusing to forgive keeps us connected to the offending person and anchored to the past. Pain and anger are divisive and can also keep people stuck, in both their corporate and personal life. When you continue to hold onto bitterness, you actually give more power to the person who hurt you. Over long periods of time, pain and anger can sometimes turn into bitterness, rage, and deep depression, and all of this can affect your health. Over time, the negative consequences of not forgiving can affect your heart rate, blood pressure, and muscles. Our bodies may also produce too much cortisol, and this keeps the cells in the body continually over-stressed.

On the other hand, forgiveness can enhance your overall health and reduce your stress. Forgiveness allows the body to be at peace and age more gracefully, as you are more at peace with yourself. As William Ward said, "Forgiveness is the key that unlocks the handcuffs of hate."[16] Forgiveness releases us from anger and resentment, and opens the door for joy to come back into our lives.

Ironically, forgiveness is both the most selfish thing you can do to free yourself, and the most unselfish thing you can do to free others. Forgiveness, like happiness, is simply a decision. The ideal situation is to forgive quickly, from the heart, and not spend another second thinking about it. As Robin Sharma writes,

> Many people bring such negative energy into their workplaces every morning because they are full of resentment and anger over past hurts and ancient betrayals … Learn to forgive the people you need to forgive and release things that happened in the past that might be consuming your precious creative potential. You can't craft a superb future by remaining stuck in your past. Because the disappointments you are holding on to are holding on to your power. By freeing yourself of them, you free up a ton of energy, passion, and potential.[17]

In summary, you will not be free without forgiveness, so never underestimate the power of humility and forgiveness. The benefits of forgiving far outweigh the consequences of not forgiving, because healing can only happen when we forgive. When we forgive and show compassion, inner torment goes away and is replaced by a feeling of peace, which has a more natural and positive impact on our work and family relationships. Remember, forgiving is the key to unlocking your inner freedom. Take it, and give yourself the gift of an enhanced quality and longevity of life in today's fast-paced, high-performance business world.

Personal finance and money

With today's fast-paced lifestyle, executives need to be in the driver's seat of managing their personal finances. Most of the following information on personal finance has been gathered over the years from industry financial experts. Similar to the section on overall physical health, I am not an expert on finance. Although some of this information can change over time, the basics remain the same. Depending on the level of financial knowledge of the particular corporate executive, this information can be helpful for learning more about your financial investments and retirement planning, and empower you to make the right financial choices for you and your family.

This book is based on the perspective of the corporate executive as a whole person. This "wholeness" is made up of aligning your vision, leadership, and wellness to achieve extraordinary success. That's The All Together Now Advantage. Personal financial health is related closely to personal wellness. However, it is also linked to personal vision and organizational leadership. The ideal spending plan starts with a personal vision of how you'd like to live right up to and including your twilight years; it all links to your desired lifestyle, quality of life, and longevity. Short- and long-term financial objectives need to match up with what's possible in eventually achieving the life of your dreams. It's about how you will achieve your personal vision financially. Personal vision, linked to organizational vision, needs to be realistic to set out the appropriate objectives to make the vision come alive.

Many executives have excellent skills for managing millions of dollars for corporations with outstanding results.

Yet, they often poorly manage their own personal finances. When managing money for corporations, it is as though they are outside the fish bowl and can see the big picture. However, when it comes to managing their own personal finances, they're often inside the fish bowl and are somehow unable to see their own big financial picture.

In most of the financial books I've read, what I've gathered is that for most self-made millionaires, being wealthy is much more about independence and freedom than it is about the money. That's why developing and articulating your personal vision is so critical. What does freedom mean to you? Does freedom mean more time for travel, more time with friends, time to write a book? Freedom means different things to different people. That's why your short- and long-term financial objectives need to be integrated with your overall personal vision, so that you set yourself up for success. It's a given that as things change over time, you need to make appropriate adjustments.

As you can well imagine, as an executive coach I've had the honour and privilege to consistently work personally, confidentially, and intensively with some of the most brilliant and successful executives in corporate North America. By building solid relationships of trust and speaking their language, including understanding what the corporate numbers mean, I have also learned much about their interests related to finance.

Exposure to such a variety of corporate executives with expertise in marketing, finance, sales, information technology, human resources, and so on, has given me invaluable exposure to what is most important in today's business world. I have often been privy to the financial implications and interests in the personal and organizational lives of the executives I coach. By actively listening to these corporate clients, I have discovered that there was a surprising pattern of significant gaps related to their specific personal-finance needs. For that reason, I further researched this topic to consolidate the critical insights for this book. For many corporate executives, these critical insights are definitely a value-add which can enhance their knowledge of personal finance.

Spending the time to take better control of your personal finances

Managing your own money should be a fundamental life skill. It's unfortunate that it was never taught in school, because the earlier in life people learn these fundamentals, the better. For some adults, there isn't anything more boring than learning how to manage their money. They simply avoid it. Yet, there's nothing more important to learn if they want financial security and freedom. I call it financial self-esteem: being in control of your own finances and having a monthly snapshot of your own value and worth. Why would you not make it a priority to get involved with managing your own money? Think about it — no one should care more about your own money than you.

Many corporate executives I know work long hours — 50, 60, or more a week. Yet, they do not spend even one hour a week carefully looking at their personal finances. Some people think a spouse, partner, son, or daughter will always be there to take care of it for them. This is playing high stakes with your hard-earned money. Why? There may come a day when you may definitely be disappointed because you didn't take more control or the time to learn more about your finances. It happens all the time, and this can create major challenges and high stress levels. Moreover, this lack of knowledge can affect our health. For some corporate executives, working long, hard hours and worrying about money can cause great emotional stress and weaken their immune system, allowing disease to invade.

We sometimes hear people say that all their problems would be solved if only they won the lottery. Yet, it's interesting that statistics show that lottery winners are often in their original or worse financial situation within a few years. To further elaborate, in *Rich Dad Poor Dad*, Robert Kiyosaki explains that money doesn't solve problems; intelligence solves problems and produces money.[18] The message is that money without financial intelligence is soon gone.

Linking money to your emotions and emotional intelligence

Personal finances are linked not only with personal vision, but also with personal leadership skills, including emotional intelligence (EQ). Think about your strategy with your own financial advisors over the last few years. Depending on the economy, investments experience peaks and valleys, similar to emotional highs and lows. There are often many pressures and questions, such as should I get out of the market now, or wait? Bob says this. Martha says that. My son says this, etc. Our expectations can be high, and when our financial returns are good, we are excited. However, when the reverse happens, we want to question our financial advisors as we begin to lose confidence. A top-notch financial advisor always keeps people focused on long-term thinking, diversifying their portfolio to maximize financial opportunities.

The personal leadership section of this book refers to Dr. Reuven Bar-On's 15 emotional competencies. Think about how directly emotional competencies link to your emotions around personal finances and money: self-regard, emotional self-awareness, assertiveness, independence, self-actualization, empathy, social responsibility, interpersonal relationships, stress tolerance, impulse control, reality testing, flexibility, problem solving, optimism, and happiness. It's obvious that being highly skilled in these emotional competencies provides a distinct advantage in understanding how money relates to your emotional intelligence. This knowledge better equips you to anticipate and understand the changes in your emotions. You are then in a better position to ask the right questions, and get the answers from your financial advisor that will provide greater clarity on your investments due to market fluctuations.

Likewise, as corporate executives enhance their knowledge of emotional intelligence, they will be able to understand better how their emotions around personal leadership affect their organizational leadership. Let's face it: when corporate executives are stressed by lower profits, and the impact on their bonuses and personal financial portfolios, the ripple effect can easily impact not only their colleagues at work, but also customer and family relationships.

What is your relationship with money? Have you ever taken the time to think about that? How do you respond emotionally to money issues? Whether it be countries at war, corporations competing, family businesses, or the family itself, relationships have been destroyed due to people's relationships with money. Are the people around you givers or takers? Do they demonstrate respect to you and others, or not? Have you ever given your family love, or your corporation respect, and they took advantage of you? You need to remember that for every choice you make, there is a consequence. If you are over-generous with your time and money, don't expect others to be as generous as you are or you will be disappointed. By clarifying your expectations around money and your relationship with money, many challenges can be prevented.

Learning more about the luxury of simplicity — how less is more

Do you know your overall value or worth? You need to articulate and write down solid objectives to be able to measure what you achieve. It's also essential to have a clear understanding not only of what your financial numbers truly are (for example, assets, liabilities, personal equity, etc.), but most importantly, what these numbers mean to your life. You need to grasp the whole picture.

For many corporate executives, success stems from paying attention to how they spend and invest their personal finances. It's interesting that many people graduate from university with all kinds of credentials, are well-trained to work in their field, and yet, sadly, are untrained to manage the money they will make in their career. In fact, when the corporate executive's goal is primarily to work for money or get rich, versus doing work about which they are passionate, their whole being can be affected, which is why personal vision is so important.

When corporate executives develop good money habits, and use these skills to care for their wealth, while maintaining the discipline to live within their means, they also naturally increase their level of financial self-esteem, self-respect, and confidence. The result is that they handle their money with wisdom and maturity, which is the key to creating and sustaining wealth. The bottom line is that there is no choice but to keep learning more about finances.

Many years ago, when I first graduated from university, a special aunt and uncle told me, "When it comes to money, Gail, always remember that it will never be about 'how much you make.' What's important is 'how much you spend,' because that's what accounts for what you have left over in the end!" At the time, it seemed like a no-brainer. Shortly after, when I moved from a small town to the big city of Toronto, I quickly learned that, although I was making an excellent salary working for a large corporation, the cost of living was much higher than in the small town. Fortunately, I never forgot those profound words. The key lesson here is never to assume that even though we are making an exceptional income, we will always be growing our finances to the next level. Whether it is being in a higher tax bracket, increased living expenses, or the purchase of other assets, what is important is what we have left over.

In North America, we live in an environment where constant advertising on television, billboards, and the Internet may lead us to believe that what we have is not enough, and that more is better. It is sometimes easy to assume that a luxury is a necessity, when it might not be. It should be more about our needs versus our wants, while enjoying what is important to us in our life.

April Lane Benson, a psychologist and editor of *To Buy or Not to Buy: Why We Overshop and How to Stop*, believes that the key is to live a richer life by redefining common notions of wealth. When gathering this research, she shared with me that, "True wealth isn't about spending. It's living your life in accordance with your values and goals with plenty of room for relationships and activities. In the end, commitment is the ultimate form of wealth."[19] Once again, in the end, it's your choice to make that commitment.

It seems to me that some people's attitude toward spending money on material things is: "I want it and I want it now." They fail to differentiate between their needs and wants, and instead look for the best "feel good" value for their money. For example, do you ever buy clothes because they are on sale and then never wear them? Or, think about this: have you bought toys for children, nieces and nephews and grandchildren rather than take them to a playground or spend some quality time with them? It's clear which is easier, but which is more important to the relationship and the child? The child will never be that age again — now they are ready for their own friends.

To this day, my most meaningful memories with uncles, aunts, and the rest of my family are what we did together. All the gifts were appreciated, but the glue in the relationships is about the memories.

Practising the cycle of giving and receiving

When corporate executives are using their excellent skills doing what they love, they reap significant compensation and rewards in salaries and bonuses. However, in my view, the most highly successful corporate executives are provided with rich inner rewards that most often transcend their monetary rewards. They get it! They understand what I call the cycle of giving and receiving; true meaningful gratification. These are the exceptional corporate executives who view both organizational and personal finances from outside the fish bowl. They look at the entire world and want to give back by contributing their time and money to bigger causes. In many cases, their philanthropy is a large part of why they are living the life of their dreams.

Philanthropic executives also understand the significance of getting and staying financially healthy. Warren Buffet, one of the richest men in the world, consistently donates millions to charity. Another philanthropist, John D. Rockefeller, was the world's only billionaire at the age of 53 in 1892. It has been said that he earned approximately a million dollars a week. At that same time, he was ill and lived on crackers and milk. He often couldn't sleep because he worried so much about his money. It's interesting that when he started giving away his money, his health changed radically for the better, and he ultimately lived to celebrate his 97th birthday. My point is that money is not the answer to your anxiety; in fact it may be the cause.

You may be thinking that these are examples of people who have amassed huge fortunes and are able to leave huge legacies, more than most corporate executives. But the point I'm trying to make is simple: it's about the cycle of giving and receiving. It's about giving back and receiving satisfaction from the giving. A legacy can be big or small. It can relate to your business, personal, or other interests. It can be a donation to a hospital, an endowment to a university or other educational institution, or a contribution to a charity that is meaningful to you. It can be giving in the form of money, property, education bursaries, volunteer activities, and so on. Many corporate executives volunteer as a board member, or share their expertise for a non-profit or charity organization. I do that myself, with great satisfaction.

As current and future consumers, we have more control than we think over how we spend our hard-earned money in relation to social responsibilities, both on a personal and corporate basis. What kind of legacy do you want to leave for your business relationships, organizations, community, and the world? How do you want to be remembered by your family and friends; how many actions of love and caring, your valued time spent with them, etc.?

The giving is the difference you will make to the community, organizations, family, etc. The receiving is the meaningful satisfaction you receive from the giving. If it is something you are incredibly passionate about, it is an even greater feeling of satisfaction and reward. In the end, the key is to practise the cycle of giving and receiving.

Having a safety net or contingency fund

Do you have a contingency fund, or what I call a "safety net"? Do you have money easily accessible to cover three to six months of living expenses if some unforeseen circumstances should occur? This could be due to a temporary job loss without benefits and perks. Or, on a happier note, it could be that unexpected opportunity for your son or daughter to participate in a special provincial or state event and you will need to have extra money available.

Be proactive in handling your legal responsibilities — Do you have a will?

Most corporate executives always have lots on their plate and can experience stress without necessarily knowing where it is coming from — it's not always from organizational concerns. Sometimes the cause is a simple act of procrastination of critical personal tasks. Are you aware of the big implications of not dealing with these important details in life? Let me share a little story with you.

Imagine that you are on a business flight from Toronto to Chicago. The airplane begins to experience terrible turbulence. The pilot announces that there will be unusual turbulence for quite some time. As the flight continues, the commotion and instability of the plane worsens. Like anyone, you get a bit shaken up and scared. This is very stressful. In fact, you aren't sure the flight will make it to Chicago. Depending on your religion or faith, you may say a few prayers. You immediately think of your spouse or partner, children, or parents. You recall that, although you had good intentions to write a will, and dearly love your family, you procrastinated and never did. You experience a flash of what life would be like on earth for them without you. What happens if you die in a plane crash?

The main point here is not about an airplane crash. It's about having a proper will. Have you procrastinated on doing the most critical task to protect your family's future? Did you know that one of the best ways you can demonstrate your love and respect to your family and loved ones is to have a will and ensure your finances are in order.

Depending on the country that you live in, be sure you meet the criteria of the regulatory bodies that govern wills. Be sure you also fulfill the appropriate legal requirements that qualify your will as being proper (i.e., executor, personal powers of attorney over your assets and for personal care).

If you have a proper will, when did you last review it? Experts in the field recommend that you review and update your will every two to three years. However, more importantly, if you marry, separate, or divorce, your will should be updated at the same time. What happens to your money when you die? Do family members or your partner or spouse, executor(s), or children know where your will and important documents are if they need to access them? Is there a particular charity about which you are passionate and to which you would like to leave money? Be sure that whoever you select to be an executor is reliable and responsible enough to carry out the duties within the appropriate timelines. You need to be assured that they will put your interests first.

On the other hand, when you take on the responsibility to be an executor for a family member or friend, ensure that you understand the responsibilities involved, so that you will be able to put the other person's interests first. You need to plan for the amount of time and commitment it takes to settle an estate. I've spoken to some retired executives who have handled large estates, and they have told me it took more than a year. As a corporate executive who is not retired and is travelling globally on business, regardless of amazing technology today, managing an estate in addition to their corporate workload can be highly stressful.

In general, the job of executor often begins with the role of power of attorney, and/or managing the finances of an elderly or palliative-care individual. Eventually you will need to be prepared to deal with the steps of funeral arrangements and other legal paperwork related to creditors, taxes, pension, beneficiaries, etc. Although you will get advice and guidance from the funeral home, and occasionally lawyers, it is an executor's job to follow through on the wishes of the deceased and every detail that goes along with it. Yes, it can be an honour and a privilege to do this for a loved one. However, know what you are getting into and what the accountabilities are.

Being proactive in selecting the right financial advisor for you

The Millionaire Mind says, "Most millionaires do not have one investment adviser — they have at least three.... Most high income people with average to above average intellect realize they aren't brilliant, but the majority have great common or practical intelligence. They know their strengths and weaknesses and act accordingly. They never make major investment decisions without first seeking advice from skilled professionals."[20]

It's important to keep in mind that there's nothing wrong with having someone handle your investments. For the most part, it is the best thing to do. What's absolutely critical is that you continue to track and monitor your investments and returns monthly to ensure there are no surprises at the end of the year, or down the road.

In her book *No Hype: The Straight Goods on Investing Your Money*, Gail Bebee says, "The successful investor is an educated investor. Even if you rely on the recommendations of a financial advisor, you need sufficient knowledge to be able to evaluate the recommendations to confirm they are in your best interests.... However, successful investing is a journey, not a destination. And ongoing investor education is part of this journey."[21]

Just like having some key knowledge of medical terminology when speaking with your doctor is advantageous, so is being familiar with key financial-investment terminology. A financial advisor is often more attentive when you are speaking their language. This can enhance your comfort level, as you make sure to ask your financial advisor the right questions to get the answers you need for your overall financial decision making. It also makes it easier for them to take financial discussions to the next level of understanding. It's fundamental that you know and understand what your portfolio is invested in. On the one hand, you absolutely need your financial advisor's advice; on the other hand, you want to be in the driver's seat of your own finances. After all, it's your money! And no one should care more about your money than you.

Take the time to learn more about financial terminology by reading money and business books and magazines. It will be worth it. Certainly, the past trends of Ponzi schemes and other unethical financial practices have created even more awareness of the importance of being directly involved in your own investment portfolio. In a nutshell, being equipped to make informed decisions about how to reach your investment goals is very important. That's because decisions related to your personal finances are directly linked to your wellness. When you are more knowledgeable and feel in control of your personal finances, you can have peace of mind and your stress can be reduced.

Over the last few years, there appears to be a lot of distrust in the financial services industry. However, trust is absolutely the key to working with a financial advisor. With so much news on Ponzi schemes, hopefully it is a huge wake-up call to all of us that any fees paid for any type of investments need to be transparent. In other words, you need to know exactly what you pay a financial advisor for the services provided. How can the financial advisor demonstrate the actual fees that you are paying? Ask them to walk you through their business processes.

Generally, most individuals spend more time researching the purchase of an entertainment centre or a car than interviewing and finding the right financial advisor. It is absolutely critical that you have a compatible relationship with your chosen financial advisor for several reasons. If you experience a crisis in your life where you are hospitalized or are unavailable, travelling abroad for instance, you need to be able to trust that your financial advisor understands your needs. Does the thought of your financial advisor handling your financial needs evoke a feeling of comfort or stress? Does the financial advisor respond quickly or procrastinate? These are important matters to think about in advance. This criteria is also important when selecting your accountant and lawyer.

Although this advice is equally as valuable for men and women, David Bach's book called *Smart Women Finish Rich*, talks about 14 Golden Rules to use when selecting a financial advisor.[22] I've repeated Bach's 14 rules word for word below. After each one, I have expanded on the rule by using a live example from my own life, how I selected my own financial advisor, John. It was a coincidence that 15 years before this book was ever published,

I had naturally gone through these steps and found them highly effective. It was reassuring to learn many years later that his recommendations matched what I did. After Bach's rules, I have also added Golden Rules 15 and 16 from my own experience.

1. **Go where the money is — Ask others with money who the names are of the Financial Advisor(s) they work with and meet and interview them.**
   I initially heard about John from a contact I met at an Executive Women's Network group in Toronto around 1990. She was impressed with his knowledge, and he had provided her with excellent services and outstanding results for several years. The following week, I called her for a more in-depth reference. I also got several additional references about him from other clients.

2. **Go to your first meeting prepared with all your information and be ready to share it if you feel comfortable.**
   I had my questions ready; however, I didn't share them with five of the eight financial advisors I met. I shared them with only three, the ones who I felt provided a strong comfort level, trust, and confidence. At this stage, I was looking for a short list of candidates. In my case, one area of my expertise is being a highly skilled professional interviewer, so I applied this skill to my advantage. You too can use a particular expertise of yours to your advantage to gather the information you need, such as interviewing, analyzing, strategizing, etc.

3. **During the first meeting, you (the client) should do most of the talking.**
   I found that this was also an important time to find

out if the financial advisor was an active listener. I asked reflective questions and had the financial advisor paraphrase them to ensure they understood what was important to me.

4. **A good Financial Advisor should be able to explain his or her investment philosophy.**

   All eight did this fairly well. However, three of them provided much greater clarity and used some story-telling techniques that helped me better understand their philosophy. It is important that you respect and are compatible with the financial advisor, and that you have a high level of comfort in communicating and sharing information with him or her. Along with the financial adviser's level of competence, trust and a high level of integrity will always be the most important parts of the service the financial advisor is offering.

   Just like with your doctor, accountant, or lawyer, it should not be stressful when you meet with your financial adviser. He or she provides a particular expertise to assist you, so be sure to deal with the right one for you.

5. **Find out what the Financial Advisor charges and how he/she is paid.**

   I checked this out, and some were based on commission and some were fee-based. I asked many questions around the positives and negatives of these choices. I needed to be assured that the financial advisor would provide complete disclosure of costs related to my return on investments. The term for that is *transparency*. Even in those days, it was challenging to get answers around transparency. Somehow banks and investment firms tend to produce statements on financial investment portfolios, for example, that are complex to read and understand. It is important to be persistent and continue to ask questions until you have clarity on all fees, including any hidden fees. Any honourable financial advisor will ensure they provide that for you; if not, find another one who will. Since the increasing incidents of the Ponzi schemes, leading-edge financial advisors are focusing on providing better transparency as a competitive edge.

6. **Decide how you want to pay your Financial Advisor**. Armed with the above information, I did some additional research to review payment options prior to my second meeting with the three short-listed financial advisors.

7. **Make yourself an important client … by saying "Thank you"**. When I received outstanding services, I referred another client to my financial advisor. I felt this was the best way to thank him.

8. **Hire a Financial Advisor with a strong support team.** When I met John, he already had an excellent support team. This included qualified back-up colleagues who could answer questions in his absence. Through him I also had access to a tax accountant, lawyer, and insurance providers, if needed, in addition to my own personal accountant, lawyer, and banker.

9. **Check out a prospective Financial Advisor's background.** Depending on the country that you live in, be sure the financial advisor you select has the appropriate credentials and licenses that meet the criteria of

the regulatory bodies that govern the industry. I
checked in advance that my financial advisor had the
appropriate credentials, a proven track-record, and a
high level of integrity.

10. **Never ever hire a Financial Advisor who brags
about his own personal performance.**
John actively listened and did not brag about his
performance. He let his references speak for themselves.

11. **A good Financial Advisor explains the risks associated
with investing.**
John was the best of the three on my short-list to be
patient and clear.

12. **Look for a Financial Advisor who has many satisfied
clients.**
With the number of references I checked, it was
apparent that John had some very satisfied clients. As
a result, I was confident that he would take the time
to understand that, for me, growing a portfolio was
about much more than money. It was about my values,
my personal vision, and what was most important
to me in the short and long term. I was committed
to ongoing growth and knowledge of finance and
investments. In other words, the quality of the service
indirectly linked to a better quality of life for me,
minimizing stress, saving time, and added confidence
that my portfolio was in good hands.

13. **Go with your gut instinct!**
As a professional interviewer, I have an intuitive
sense. What's key here is to both do your homework
and use your gut instinct.

14. **Keep in regular contact with your Financial Advisor.**
John and I meet at least twice a year and speak when
required to make any appropriate changes to my
financial investment strategies.

The next two Golden Rules are my added recommendations,
and go beyond Bach's list.

15. **The Financial Advisor should be about five to 10
years younger than the client.**
As I get older, I continually need a financial advisor. I
believe, where possible, a long term close relationship
helps the financial advisor make the right key financial
decisions for a client right into their golden years.

16. **Life happens! Don't take anything for granted —
especially your Financial Advisor. Over time, be
aware of any key changes in their behaviour or
financial reporting and question it.**
Are they taking your business for granted? Are they
still meeting regularly with you to keep you informed?
Does your financial advisor still remain a good fit
for working with you? All of this is a journey, not a
destination. We have choices along the way.

Broaden your knowledge and perspective by keeping abreast of financial trends

Financial information and trends constantly evolve, so it is
important to stay abreast of new information from a broad
perspective. For example, Dan Richards, president of Strategic
Imperatives, shares that there has been "a shift in mindset" related to the kinds of questions that investors are now asking.
Richards says:

In conversations with investors, there's often a generational divide on this issue. Canadians in their late 60s, 70s and 80s are more likely to operate the way they always did, deferring to their adviser to take the lead on their portfolios. On the other hand, younger investors are increasingly assertive about the questions they ask and are looking to collaborate on decision making. Until recently, these investors would often respond to a recommendation with, "If that's what you think, fine."[23]

In short, for today's generation, conversations with financial advisors are taking longer and investors are asking tougher questions.

Further, today's investors tune into various sites on the internet for financial information. They are interested in reviewing information from multiple sources from various viewpoints. Richards shares further, "For good or ill, we live in a world that's moving to shorter and shorter attention spans.... As we move into 2010, investors need to have candid conversations with their advisers about the information they are looking for — both what they get and how they get it. Only in that way will investors get the value they're paying for — and only in that way will the adviser-client relationships be sustainable."[24]

Summarizing key learning for financial investing

In his book *Gimme My Money Back*, Ali Velshi, CNN's chief business correspondent, says, "Very few investors have the time, the tools or the know-how to perform the analysis required to optimize their own portfolios. But any portfolio, except those that are already optimal, can be made more efficient through careful, disciplined asset allocation. This is an area where a professional advisor — a good one — can add value."[25]

Below is a summary of Velshi's key learnings, in his words:

1. **Risk and return go together.** We learned that it's necessary to accept some risk if we want to beat inflation and build wealth. We also learned that each asset class has its own risk and reward characteristics.

2. **Time is your friend.** We saw that time smoothes the effects of volatility, allowing each asset class to produce its expected long-term returns.

3. **Diversification can help provide more predictable returns.** We saw that, because asset classes don't all move in lockstep, diversification lowers portfolio risk overall. When stocks are down, for example, bonds may be up. So a portfolio with both stocks and bonds produces more consistent earnings than either asset alone.

4. **Asset allocation is your most important portfolio decision.** We learned that asset allocation — the process of dividing your investment among many different kinds of assets — is the key to performance. As we noted, some studies suggest that asset allocation is responsible for more than 90 percent of the difference in returns between portfolios. It's far more important than individual stock or bond selection and market timing combined.

5. **You can optimize your portfolio to get the lowest risk for the return you want.** We examined the efficient frontier, that hypothetical curve that gives you the return you want for the least possible risk.[26]

Gail Bebee has a way of saying it simply and clearly. Her five universal rules of investing are: "1) Think for yourself; 2) Know yourself; 3) Manage your risk; 4) Be patient; 5) Be decisive… Above all, don't forget that life is for living and successful investing provides a means to live your life the way you want."[27]

I mentioned earlier that over the years, I've been privy to both the personal and organizational financial implications and interests of many corporate executives. This unique opportunity has allowed me to highlight some critical insights on personal finance here. For many corporate executives, these critical insights are the missing links for them to enhance their knowledge around personal finance and help reduce their stress.

In summary, it's about spending the time to take better control of your finances so you can understand more about how money links to your emotional intelligence. Further, it's critical to learn more about the luxury of simplicity — less is more. Practise the cycle of giving and receiving; you'll find that it brings you significant rewards. Have a safety net or contingency fund, and have a proper will that is updated every two to three years. When selecting a financial advisor, practise the 16 Golden Rules. And finally, broaden your knowledge and perspective by keeping abreast of financial trends, while remembering Ali Velshi's fundamental five key lessons and Gail Bebee's five universal rules of investing. Practising these critical insights has big payoffs, not only for your personal finances, but for your overall personal wellness.

I intentionally positioned the section on personal finances at the end of the Personal Wellness section, as you can see that it brings the Model on Total Balance and Integration of vision, leadership and wellness full circle, back to your personal vision. I call this The All Together Now Advantage. It requires your personal-finance plan to get you moving toward achieving your personal vision.

In conclusion, lifestyle management is a broad term that encompasses many important elements. I have included sections on work/life balance, managing stress, image consulting, happiness, forgiveness, and personal finances because these are the areas I have found to be of the most critical significance for the executives I coach. What keeps you healthy? What are the elements you need to focus on most in your life? I have witnessed many of my corporate-executive clients make the kind of behaviour changes it takes to deepen their personal wellness and further strengthen their lifestyle management, and thus facilitate their success in both their personal and professional life. With Courage, Choice, and Commitment, you can do the same.

CHAPTER SEVEN

Organizational Wellness

PLANTING THE SEEDS OF INTEGRATING WELLNESS WITH VISION AND LEADERSHIP — HOW IT ALL STARTED

In the early years of my career, I worked at a large consumer packaged goods corporation in Canada. As part of my human resources responsibilities, I recruited high potential candidates in universities across Canada to be further trained, developed, and groomed for senior level positions for the organization in years to come. At that time, I also began to design programs, which were then called stress-management programs. This was critical for meeting the needs of so many managers who were working long hours, achieving promotions, and climbing up the ladder of success, yet burning out. I wanted to understand the impact of stress on the body, as I witnessed its negative impacts in some of the people who worked for the organization. So, a small group of other passionate employees and I made a number of presentations to the presidential team. Finally, we were able to get the support and approval of the president at head office, along with the president of one of the major subsidiaries, to pay for several of us to go to night school to study anatomy and physiology, and learn more about bringing fitness into the organization. I was then trained to become a certified fitness instructor, and volunteered my services to teach fitness at lunch hours for seven years.

Let me share a story with you from my life in the early 1980s. In addition to my role in human resources, I would regularly join the executive team halfway through a long meeting in the boardroom to lead them in a 15-minute stretch and fitness break to get the blood flowing. In those days, I brought along a portable tape recorder to make it quick and easy. A few of the executives would stay at the back of the room, not participating. Instead, they laughed and chuckled at the apparent silliness of it all. Interestingly enough, the ones who were curious and open to learning more about fitness and health are now movers and shakers as highly regarded CEOs in corporate North America. I will be forever grateful to those senior managers and executives who supported me and our fitness team to be one of the first corporations in Canada to invest in an on-site fitness centre.

My experience at that organization was the first major step in my passion to promote organizational wellness, and to integrate it with vision and leadership. As an organization development specialist, I began to design and incorporate health and wellness into core management development programs, connecting the balance of life with increased productivity and return on human assets for the organizations I worked with. I was one of the first corporate organization development specialists in Canada to spearhead the promotion of fitness in the corporate environment in the early 1980s. It was a bold move, with minimum support in the initial stages. At the time, the idea that stress management and fitness could be highly cost effective and positively impact productivity and profits was unheard of.

The support of the president at head office, along with the president of one of the major subsidiaries, planted the seed for the approach I take in my current coaching practice. This truly was the beginning of my integration of wellness with vision and leadership. The fruit of that seed eventually turned into The All Together Now Advantage and the reason for this book today.

Do you work for an organization that respects work/life balance, provides a fitness center or fitness subsidies, and has healthy food in the cafeteria? This combination is so essential for both you and your staff: it is difficult to focus on maximizing your productivity when your brain isn't equipped with proper nutrients. You need to be able to concentrate on achieving the day-to-day results that accumulate into achieving quarterly and annual outstanding business results. In a nutshell, it's about healthy people working in healthy organizations to achieve healthy profits. It's that simple.

WHO IS RESPONSIBLE FOR ORGANIZATIONAL WELLNESS?

When an executive has developed and articulated his personal vision, and links it to the organizational vision, has outstanding personal and organizational leadership skills, is in good shape, and healthy, organizational wellness is simply what I call the "icing on the cake." But, who is responsible for organizational wellness?

Sometimes corporate executives think that the human resources department's function is to be responsible and accountable for organizational wellness. Human resources is often involved in researching topics related to organizational wellness — especially in leading-edge organizations. More importantly, it is the role of human resources to strategically position organizational wellness. However, it is the CEO and the entire senior management executive team who are responsible and accountable for organizational wellness, from buying into the concept to supporting organizational wellness and being role models in integrating their decisions into the day-to-day operations of the organization.

WHY ORGANIZATIONAL WELLNESS IS KEY TO YOUR LONG-TERM SUCCESS AND SURVIVAL

Just as a successful organization needs to be healthy and resilient, so does each executive leader need to be healthy and resilient. In short, a senior management team of healthy executives is good business. It can directly sustain performance results in the long term.

In these modern, technological times, many products and services are so competitive that, in the end, the true edge in organizations is the people — the corporate executives, their team and staff. Organizations lose billions of dollars every year because of stress-related illnesses. The top three causes of sickness and death in the United States are related to lifestyle: high fat diet, lack of exercise, and smoking. With a greater focus on health and wellness, there is often a lower cost related to health care in the organization. By integrating wellness into an organization, it helps employees to gradually change unhealthy behaviours, and employers to reduce health-care costs, while promoting a healthier and more productive work force.

Healthy employees who manage their stress require less organization dollars spent on their health and benefit programs. When employees are highly stressed, it can lead to more absenteeism, sickness, and medical drugs, and eventually to short-term disability, long-term disability, and so on. This is a major challenge in the twenty-first century, and much of it is due to the juggling home and work responsibilities. That is why progressive organizations understand that their top priority is taking care of their people, and supporting them from an organizational wellness perspective.

Some of the trends that are making corporations take a closer look at being increasingly supportive of organizational wellness relate to the rising costs of health care and prescription drugs, along with how the technological revolution has created new health concerns, such as repetitive strain and stress injuries. Organizations are becoming educated on how providing health-related workshops can get the staff more informed to prevent potential illnesses and the costs related to issues such as poor nutrition, excess alcohol consumption, smoking, or a sedentary lifestyle.

In today's fast-paced business world, life is a blur between work and home. Executives at work may be stressed by their boss, direct reports, or a group of staff in a specific department with conflicting viewpoints. Or they may be stressed at home with a spouse, partner, or family member, sometimes even going through a separation or divorce. Or they may just simply be overworked and stressed out with too many hours of overtime and not enough physical activity or sleep. Whether you are under stress at home or at work, when you switch environments, your stress carries over. Many people spend more of the wakeful hours at work than at home. If the environment at work is not a healthy one, it wreaks havoc with their health and their ability to be a high performer.

Keeping executives, their team, and their staff healthy is best done when the organization "practises what it preaches" by staying true to its vision and values, and providing support for corporate executives and their staff. If asked, can you instantly share the vision and values of your organization? How often do you emphasize and verbalize how your strategies and key projects link to the vision and values of the organization, particularly those that are directly linked with staff issues and organizational wellness? If you stopped one of your staff in the hallway at work, could they tell you with passion what the vision and values are? Are your staff aware of words in your vision such as "respect, high energy level, strength" etc. that relate to organizational wellness? Are you a consistent role model? I find it interesting that, sometimes in the first coaching session, executives will need to refer to their organization's website or a file in their desk drawer to share their organizations vision and values. For this information, I want the passion, not the print. I want it to be something that is such a part of them that they never have to look it up. To truly live out organizational wellness and be a role model in your organization, it has to be a part of your fabric, both personally and professionally.

When joining any corporation that promotes itself as being committed to organizational wellness, the big question is always, "Does the organization put its money where its mouth is?" Before you join an organization, it is up to you to do your due diligence. The ideal is that there are no surprises after joining the firm. Likewise, the organization needs to do its due diligence in the selection process to ensure that the corporate executive not only has the knowledge and skills to excel, but also has a positive, healthy attitude and is a good fit for the organization, that they are supportive of wellness and will be a role model for staff.

Another key to supporting organizational wellness is that CEOs and key corporate executives are major human assets to an organization. That is why the whole executive team shouldn't fly together, even in a private jet. In the event of a tragedy, too much knowledge and private information would be lost all at one time. CEOs are often so connected to the brand and performance of the organization that their departure, or word of their potential departure from the organization, can instantly and negatively impact the stock price index for the shares of that organization. In 2009, for example, news broke on Steve Jobs's major health issues. Jobs, the CEO of Apple Inc., is such a central part of Apple's brand, that his private health issues became public knowledge. The CEO himself had become a major core asset of the organization.

In general, the new generation is taking more of an active interest in improving their health. Moreover, they seek organizations that are willing to support and invest in health care. In fact, the new generation is familiar with the phrase "our health is our wealth." As a result, it is now even more of a priority for progressive organizations to not only provide executive coaching services for leadership development, but also to provide executive coaching services in lifestyle management and wellness in attracting and retaining top talent.

The new generation makes decisions to move elsewhere "with their feet." If they are not satisfied with work/life balance and a health-oriented work environment, they will move to organizations that provide the supports required. These supports include leadership development and executive coaching, when appropriate, to keep them marketable and accelerating their performance with a desire to stay and continue to be engaged. So you can see, they are looking for much more than the amount of the weekly paycheque. To attract these highly talented executives, it is important that organizations be proactive and set the stage for a work environment that promotes wellness.

WHAT AREAS MAKE THE DIFFERENCE FOR ORGANIZATIONAL WELLNESS

Patrick Lencioni's book, *The Three Signs of a Miserable Job*, says that anonymity, irrelevance, and immeasurement are the three underlying factors that can make any job in any industry a misery for the employee. Without addressing each of these three areas, and promoting an environment for organizational wellness, staff will eventually leave an organization and go elsewhere. This has huge costs for the organization, since they then have to recruit, train, and further develop new people to take the place of those who have left.

Staff members need to be known and appreciated for the unique qualities they offer an organization. Each person has a distinctive set of gifts, skills, expertise, and experience to offer the organization. This is true for each corporate executive, and also for each member of their team and staff.

Further, staff members need to know that what they are doing makes a difference. When people feel stuck and like their work doesn't matter, they will resign and move to another organization that will better appreciate them. Most people have a need to be recognized and supported, not only for their work inside the organization, but also from a whole-person perspective. They want the organization to appreciate their interests and involvement related to social responsibilities, green environment projects, community involvements, supporting disaster relief projects, and other charities.

And finally, staff need to be able to assess and measure their progress. More than ever, it is critical for corporate North America to have solid formal performance management systems. Staff who are highly committed to their work always want to be kept in the loop so that they can perform and achieve their objectives. The new generation is more demanding than ever to be given feedback and kept informed, not only about what they have done, but also about where they are going, and their career development within the organization. They want to have stretch goals to stay marketable, and be measured and paid according to their worth. They are saying, "It's not what you did for me five years ago. It's about what you are doing for me today." On the same note, most are excited to step outside of their comfort zone to participate in training, development, and coaching to take their skill set to a whole new level. In this way, they can demonstrate their new-found knowledge and skills to the organization.

Executives need to provide their staff with the fundamentals of a meaningful job, which will naturally sustain their motivation. This includes more than a job description; it includes communication about the clarity and expectations around the job, and also having meaningful performance reviews where there is discussion about goals related to their career path, for further growth in areas jointly agreed upon. That's all a part of organizational wellness and being a good leader. A healthy work environment needs to be nurtured, which requires people-management skills and the time required to work with staff. When there is excellent communication and active listening with individual team members and staff, there is less stress in the work environment.

Lencioni writes, "In a work of ubiquitous technology and rapid dissemination of information, it is harder and harder to establish sustainable competitive advantage through strategic and tactical decision making. Cultural differentiation, however, is more valuable than it's ever been, because it requires courage and discipline more than creativity or intelligence."[1]

To set themselves apart, organizations need to develop a culture of organizational wellness and fulfillment. Whether it's a promotion up the ladder or a move to a functional position with broader scope, senior managers and corporate executives want to grow and stay marketable. In many cases, the trends indicate that managers and executives today will work in a number of organizations and will have several different careers in their lifetimes. Meaningful jobs are becoming much more of an attraction than monetary rewards.

Attitude surveys and 360 Feedback are standard proactive tools used in organizations today that can help take the pulse of the morale, comfort, and distress levels of the entire organization. It is especially helpful for the organization to deal with morale issues in the early stages. Some leading-edge organizations customize the attitude survey and 360 Feedback tools to incorporate many key aspects of organizational wellness. The results provide excellent insights to further support and help set the executive, his team and staff, and the organization up for success. Most progressive organizations regularly use the attitude survey to monitor feedback on the corporate benefits provided to ensure these meet the overall needs of the staff.

When it comes to organizational wellness, there are several key areas that can make the difference and a positive impact in the quality of a corporate executive's life, their team, and staff. These are areas that can support ongoing productivity, as well as sustain the momentum of a successful organization. When an organization is practising organizational wellness effectively, the corporate executive is fairly and competitively compensated according to industry standards for the value of the work being done. It also means that the organization provides best practices, such as solid health benefits, including a fitness center or subsidized fitness programs, Employee Assistance Programs, training and development, career transition assistance if the employee is downsized, and so on. This type of support helps take the corporate executive and his staff to a whole new quality of life in sustaining wellness. Working in a healthy environment, with positive morale directly impacts productivity and profits.

To make Canada's Top 100 Employers list, organizations are rated on the basis of eight different categories: physical workplace; work atmosphere and social; health, financial, and family benefits; vacation and time off; employee communications; performance management; training and skills development; and community involvement. These categories are a good match for what most corporate executives look for in organizational wellness.

Let me highlight two broad areas that cover many of these categories: executive compensation packages and work/life balance. Within these areas, I also want to draw attention to changing demographics, and how the interests and demands of the new generation must influence our approach to organizational wellness.

Organizational wellness and executive compensation programs

The corporate executive with high self-esteem, who is highly knowledgeable in his or her field of expertise, with excellent leadership skills, will want to be paid according to his or her value and worth. Integrating wellness into executive compensation programs can create a positive impact on the overall health and productivity of the executive, as well as the organization's bottom line. As executives become more educated on wellness, they can champion the integration of health activities into the work culture. This high level of ongoing support often leads to a changing mindset toward the importance of wellness.

Keep in mind that the objective of any total compensation and benefit program is to attract the best executives, remain competitive, increase job satisfaction, control costs, reduce turnover, enhance employee security and increase employee morale, and, of course, reward superior performance.

In general, successful compensation models define the total compensation philosophy and link it directly with the overall organizational vision, mission, strategies, and objectives. Commitment, support, and role modelling from the senior management team are key for the long-term successful integration of wellness into an organization's culture and executive compensation and benefit programs. Wellness initiatives should be encouraged for all employees, not just the more athletic fitness folks.

Developing a total compensation philosophy — what questions should organizations ask?

When an executive compensation and benefit program is established, it's critical to communicate the commitment and expectations to executives, and ensure clarity on the "how tos" of measuring the success of compensation and benefits programs. Some key questions that progressive organizations need to ask prior to developing the total compensation philosophy for corporate executives, especially related to wellness, include: What will the total compensation program accomplish from a wellness perspective for executives and all levels of management? Does the "intent to pay for performance" include a long-term commitment related to the wellness of executives versus a performance-only focus, which can potentially cause burnout? How does the executive compensation and benefit program compare to the competition? Will executives share in the cost of the benefits? What wellness services will be provided?

Although wellness programs were once perceived as a perk that only large corporations were able to offer, attracting and retaining highly talented executives today is critical. This process revolves around the many factors of keeping executives happy and productive, such as a healthy working environment, a good benefits package, and time for themselves and their families. Today's high performing executive needs to maintain a healthy body *and* a sharp mind, as well as a balance between work and family.

Although organizations can provide wellness services, often only a small percent of executives use them — that is until the mindset and behaviours in the culture begin to change. Considering that wellness programs usually make up a small portion of organization health care expenses, these initiatives make a lot of sense when looking at the bottom line. They demonstrate that an organization, by following through in investing in employee health, makes a strong message and impression to attract and retain executives.

Specific corporate benefits that promote wellness

Beyond normal benefit coverage, corporate benefits should also include, where possible, elements that promote wellness, such as private medical or annual physicals, a corporate fitness center or subsidized fitness programs, and the option to use hotels with fitness facilities when travelling on business, as well as a cafeteria providing nutritious and healthy food choices, including specific foods to meet the needs of people with diabetes or other particular healthy meal requests, and customized workshops on ongoing health education.

Other benefits linked to reducing stress levels include concierge services, massage therapy, elder-care support services, educational assistance, financial services, including tax and estate planning, flexible spending accounts, company cars, home security services, day-care, family leave initiatives, and compensation for travel and entertainment.

Most of the larger organizations provide an employee assistance program through a third party where the executive or his staff can, confidentially, have their needs met with specific services such as counselling related to alcoholism, smoking cessation, divorce, bereavement, contacts for elder care, day care issues for children, as well as high-stress issues with children (such as autism).

Many organizations provide flex benefits so that both the seasoned and younger generation of executives and staff can select the type of benefits that best fit their specific needs. These might include medical/dental (physiotherapy, massage therapy, acupuncture, vision care, dental, etc.); vacation; sick plans (short- and long-term disability); and personal leave policies (maternity, paternity, sabbaticals).

From an organizational-wellness perspective, my experience has been that most large organizations will provide private medical services for corporate executives to have their annual physical. These senior executives are key assets to the business, and critical to its sound success, so it is a worthwhile investment to support these executives in proactive health care.

Just as executives need to be responsible for managing their wellness and taking charge of their health, organizations also need to provide the supportive environment to sustain these changes. Some corporations are replacing the annual physical checkup they provide with enrollment in a preventative health-care program at a private medical centre. Some of them offer sophisticated and comprehensive medical programs to those interested in wellness (preventing illness), rather than illness care. They usually have a wide range of executive health programs and preventative medical programs and impressive benefits. This includes an individualized health plan, working with a physician, nutritionist, and fitness expert. The health progress of the executive is monitored and the therapies include traditional Western medical treatments, naturopathic, homeopathic, and traditional Chinese medicine.

Vacation benefits

In terms of vacation time, we need to remember that the word vacation means "vacate," and not "being at work" while we are "on vacation." Smart organizations ensure that their staff can detach from the office while on vacation so that they can be re-energized when they return. If they get burned out, both the executive and the organization lose.

The corporate executive who is a good leader and masters lifestyle management and overall wellness, needs to be a role model not only of taking vacation themselves, but also ensuring their staff takes regular vacation. This includes making the appropriate lifestyle management and overall wellness decisions for staff when an employee may need some personal time. If they have solid objectives set for their employees and the employee is consistently meeting and exceeding them, there is great leverage from a productivity perspective for the organization to be flexible to the needs of the employee taking some personal time when appropriate.

In summary, the current shortage of executive talent and leaders is the single most critical issue facing organizations. Therefore, it makes good business sense for organizations to look at compensation with a "broader" view to include non-cash compensation initiatives aimed at promoting preventative-wellness initiatives above and beyond the traditional reactive medical treatments, especially at the executive level.

SUPPORTING WORK/LIFE BALANCE

Today's executives have a different work ethic and loyalty than the previous generation. Many of them witnessed their parents get the "pink slip" after 25 to 30 years of loyalty to an organization. In many cases, to the detriment of their health and families, their reward was burnout and poor health. This generation wants to avoid the same fate as their parents. In order to adapt to the values and expectations of the upcoming generation, organizations need to be more flexible and adaptable, listen more actively, and understand that their value set is very different from the previous generation. This younger generation of executives has been brought up as the center of attention, and have no intention of putting themselves through the type of self-sacrificing their parents did for them when they were children.

Today, an exceptionally knowledgeable and talented executive leader wants to contribute his or her efforts to an environment where there is a healthy return on the energy and time invested. Highly marketable executives select the organization that supports overall wellness: a healthy and positive work environment, flexibility of time for family needs and personal health needs, as well as competitive salaries and compensation programs. They understand that they need wellness in both their careers and family life.

The desire for more time for self and family is a hot intangible commodity for corporate executives. Nothing can replace spending time with family, especially when they have young children. This is often driven by the rise of the dual-career family, where there's a need to juggle responsibilities in the home and at work. More and more couples are taking maternity and paternity leave to spend precious time with their children. In fact, many family physicians have noticed that men are taking much more of an active role in child rearing and assisting with elderly parents. More and more fathers are bringing their children to their regular medical checkups. There are also more stay-at-home dads, who are enjoying nurturing their children, which was a role previously occupied more by the mother.

Executives today are more health conscious and educated about health issues. They are more knowledgeable and better equipped to understand and appreciate the value of integrating work/life balance to attain a high quality of life. They want to be healthy and active in their later years to reap the benefits of their hard work, to enjoy their children and grandchildren, to travel, and so on. They also understand the strong link between work/life balance and sustaining high levels of performance at work to achieve extraordinary success. Yet, they are often pulled in many different directions by competing obligations. They need to establish boundaries between work and home life, their active social life, and sports and hobbies.

Organizations are finally realizing that it is in their own best business interests to have more flexible arrangements to accommodate employees when things like an emergency with a sick child or an elderly parent happen. When employees are that distressed, they can't focus on the job anyway. Many years ago, I had an excellent executive assistant working for me. Whenever her young child had to be home sick, I knew it was too difficult for her not to be with her child. So she would start work later and leave earlier for a few days. Because of our relationship and respect for each other, I was confident that when her daughter felt better, she would ensure that everything was caught up at the office and she would more than make up for the time lost — and she always did. From this you can see that not only is the managerial relationship key to providing a supportive working environment, there needs to be excellent communication programs for employees to very clearly comprehend the benefits and services available.

Organizations with a strong wellness value will extend their initiatives to include protocols around the use of BlackBerrys and other portable communication devices. This technology was designed to make communication more efficient and instantaneous, especially for those whose positions require frequent travel. The expectation should not be that the employee with one of these devices is available 24/7, as this runs counter to the concepts of individual wellness and work/life balance. These devices can promote a culture of "workaholism," which is not sustainable, either individually or organizationally, especially given the values and beliefs of many of the current generation and virtually all of the next generation of leaders.

Leading-edge organizations are being proactive in attracting high-calibre talent by providing everything from family-friendly wellness programs to policies and support programs related to work/life balance. They understand that when they respect the work/life balance of corporate executives and their staff, it increases productivity and profit. It makes good business sense.

IN CONCLUSION

When the organization hires a corporate executive or other staff, it is hiring the *whole* person. Whatever challenges or problems that person faces can directly or indirectly impact the culture, teams, and performance within the organization. The staff member needs an excellent skill set that matches the key competencies for the job, he or she needs to be naturally motivated and engaged in the position, and an excellent fit for the culture of the organization. To attract top talent, it is increasingly important to provide a broad spectrum of benefits. It is also critical that organizational culture and behaviours support work/life balance. Current demographics are changing, and complex global markets demand more sophisticated leadership skills and cultural sensitivity. By developing leading-edge compensation programs that integrate wellness, organizations can be highly supportive and influential in positively impacting the talent-management strategies and solutions of the organization in the twenty-first century.

Quality leadership will also be a key factor in organizational success in the twenty-first century. Only those organizations that get their executive compensation right will be able to attract and retain the key executives they need to be competitive. Integrating wellness into executive-compensation programs that are aligned with key organizational strategies is a proactive approach required for organizations to excel in facing this growing competition in the global marketplace.

My coaching experiences have strongly supported the notion that when executives experience a high level of satisfaction in their careers, including personal growth, health, financial rewards, and time for family and friends, recreation and relaxation, they are better able to maximize skills and potential, and apply them on the job. Imagine this. You are in great physical shape and feel good. You have a partner or spouse, family, and friends that matter to you. You have time for yourself and time for them. You excel at work and you enjoy developing your successors. Your results have incredible impact on the organization. Your organization continues to be a leader in the field. You go to work with passion, and you come home with passion. You find time for your hobby, sports, fitness, and other interests. You love life every day! You have more to give to others, yet it does not seem like you need to expend all of your energy. You have more time for community involvement, and the more you give, the better you naturally feel. You are so engaged and empowered that your enthusiasm is contagious to others. In fact, your staff comes to you as a leader; they consistently asks what they can do to perform better for you. The needs of the whole person are met to support the pursuit of both your intellectual and physical well-being. This is the direction you want to be headed for.

Research shows that highly marketable executives want to work for organizations that support leadership development and wellness coaching services, workshops related to nutrition and fitness, career development programs, and so on. They also want to work for organizations that support overall wellness, a healthy and positive working environment, flexibility of time for family needs, personal health needs, and competitive salaries. They understand that they need wellness in both their career and family life.

The role of the organization is to provide development, which enables executives to stay marketable and work in a healthy environment so that the executive, in turn, will demonstrate a high level of performance for the organization. The role of the executive is to take full advantage of the benefits provided to significantly contribute to the organization — it's a win-win.

CONCLUSION

The All Together Now Advantage

ALIGNING VISION, LEADERSHIP, AND WELLNESS TO ACHIEVE EXTRAORDINARY SUCCESS

Extraordinary success comes from mastering and aligning vision, leadership, and wellness.

The foundation is our unique and authentic personal vision. Once you discover and articulate that personal vision for yourself, you no longer have to keep searching for it. Keep it simple. What's your personal vision? Are you living it daily? Are you living the life of your dreams, or are you a corporate executive who is missing that crucial piece of information that "ignites" your life and takes it to a whole new level? Your personal vision needs to be an excellent match with your organizational vision. When your personal vision is not aligned with your organizational vision, your stress levels will increase. Remember, you spend most of your time and energy in the workplace, so if your vision and values are a good fit with the workplace, it will be more meaningful for you.

As a leader, you must live out your personal and organizational vision. Exceptional leaders continually work at developing all six key leadership competencies: strategic thinking; communication, especially active listening; emotional intelligence; negotiating and conflict management; managing energy and time; and mastering lifestyle management and overall wellness. Then, they apply these leadership competencies in their organization by inspiring others in the direction the organization needs to go, creating an excellent learning environment, and being a role model to their team and staff. They do all this with integrity and humility, with a high level of self-awareness and an understanding of how their behaviour impacts others.

If vision ignites, and leadership develops and acts, wellness sustains. More than ever, the world needs highly talented visionaries, leaders, and role models of wellness. Corporate executives need to maximize their potential and achieve a better balance of wellness to feel more fulfilled. On a personal level, wise executives are attentive to managing all aspects of both their physical health and lifestyle. They embrace the luxury of simplicity. Moreover, on an organizational level, the most progressive and successful organizations have wellness as a fundamental part of their values and practices.

In the fast-paced world of the twenty-first century today, I wholeheartedly believe that as more and more corporate executives learn how to align their personal and organizational vision, leadership, and wellness, they will achieve extraordinary success for themselves and their organizations. This is The All Together Now Advantage. It means healthy corporate executives, healthy staff, and healthy profits.

ASSESSING YOUR AREAS OF STRENGTH AND NEED FOR FURTHER DEVELOPMENT

Being equipped with information about the importance of aligning your vision, leadership, and wellness to achieve extraordinary success is the first step to making small or big changes. What is the "missing piece" keeping you from living the life of your dreams?

In my coaching practice, I mainly use psychometric tools that are scientifically validated. However, let me offer you two very general self-assessment tools as a starting place. The first helps you diagnose how performance and wellness interconnect in your life. To use the matrix below, first consider your performance. Would you rate yourself a low, medium, or high performer in your current position? Then, consider your overall wellness and work/life balance. Would you rate it low, medium or high? Then, find the square on the matrix that appears to fit you best.

Leadership and Wellness Self-Diagnostic Tool

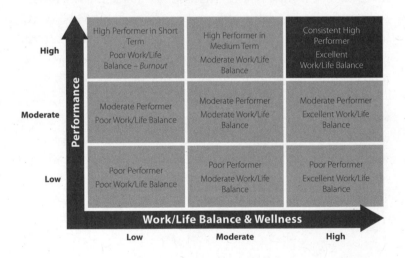

What this matrix illustrates so powerfully is how strongly performance and wellness are interconnected. You may consider yourself a high performer. However, match high performance with a low level of work/life balance and wellness, and your long-term performance will be compromised. In fact, high-performance plus a low level of work/life balance and wellness is a recipe for burnout. Instead, the ideal place you want to be is in the top right corner, demonstrating high performance that is consistent in the long term, along with excellent work/life balance and wellness.

The second self-assessment tool called Identifying Areas of Growth, helps benchmark your marketability to achieve extraordinary success. First, rate yourself on each of the three elements — vision, leadership, and wellness — on a scale of 1 to 10. A rating of 1 is not very effective, while a rating of 10 is highly effective. Your areas of strength are the ones where you rate yourself 8 or more. Any score less than 8 is an area that requires development.

When you have rated each area, multiply each of your ratings by each other. This is your All Together Now Advantage Index. The maximum score would be 10 x 10 x 10, for a total of 1,000.

When you multiply your score in each element together, what is your All Together Now Advantage Index? How do you think you compare with other corporate executives?

If your total score is 600 or greater, congratulations! You need to work on refining and tweaking the key areas that can bring you to peak performance. It won't take that much effort; you are almost there.

If your total score is between 400 and 599, you need to decide which category (vision, leadership, or wellness) you want to focus most of your effort on to get the greatest return on investment for energy expended.

If your total score is between 200 and 399, there is plenty of work to do. You need to consider working with an executive coach who has the appropriate expertise to assist you to get on track to achieve your desired outcomes.

If your total score is below 200, you are way outside the benchmark. This is serious and requires a specific plan to further develop and integrate your skills in all three areas if you have any desire to compete for corporate executive positions in the twenty-first-century marketplace.

Both of these tools, the Leadership and Wellness Self-Diagnostic Tool and the Identifying Areas of Growth Tool, can be a starting point to help you identify your areas of strength, and the areas where you need to develop. So, what next?

WHAT WILL YOUR LEGACY BE?

You are a unique human being, a corporate executive who has much to contribute to your professional life in organizations, your personal life with your family and friends, as well as to your country and the world. How you live your life will make a difference. You can learn to accomplish The All Together Now Advantage right now and live the life of your dreams. You need to decide what you want your legacy to be.

It is a universal human desire to live a fulfilling life. Have you defined through your own personal vision what true fulfillment means to you? I have learned that it is helpful to listen to older and wiser people. I have often asked them what they would do differently if they could live their lives over again. Many of them said they would have spent more time working on their relationships. They wished they would have laughed more, and taken many things less seriously. Most of them said they would have taken more risks. Many said they were glad they took the risks they did, as it took them out of their comfort zone to grow beyond their wildest expectations.

By writing this book, I have endeavored to make it as easy as possible for you to learn more about the importance of aligning vision, leadership, and wellness to achieve extraordinary success and live the life of your dreams. Now it is your turn to act, to take the next brave steps to maximize and fulfill your potential by applying what you've learned here to the areas you need to further develop in your own life.

This book is my humble offering toward that dream, both for yourself and your organization. By aligning vision, leadership, and wellness in both your professional and personal life, you can accomplish so much more while expending much less energy. It takes Choice, Courage, and Commitment, but it will be well worth it. You will have more time for family, more time for golf, for tennis, for sailing — whatever you love to do and whatever your passions. And, you'll be living the life of your dreams.

In your quest to optimize who you are and learn more about living the life of your dreams, this book can serve as your foundation. Aligning vision, leadership, and wellness is the framework to help you to make the best of your life, as you journey toward improving the quality of your life, as well as your longevity. You already have a vast amount of knowledge. You may simply need a top-notch executive coach to help you extract some of this wisdom and bring it all together for you in your personal and professional context.

Embrace life. Appreciate it! Life is precious so never take it for granted. My wish for you as an individual and corporate executive is to live a more meaningful and gratifying life, leaving behind a strong legacy. I want you to maximize your performance while achieving a better balance in life. I want you to live The All Together Now Advantage.

NOTES

CHAPTER 1 — Personal Vision

1. Harold Kushner, *How Good Do We Have to Be?: A New Understanding of Guilt and Forgiveness* (USA: Little, Brown and Company, 2006), 162.
2. Brian Klemmer, *If How-To's Were Enough, We'd All be Skinny, Rich and Happy* (USA: Vision Imprints Publishing, 2005), Audio book, Chapter 5.
3. *Ibid.*
4. Stephen Covey, *The 7 Habits of Highly Effective People* (New York: Free Press, 2004).
5. Barbara De Angelis, *Real Moments* (New York: Dell Publishing, 1994), 126.
6. Robert Straby, comments on Srully Blotnick, *The Life Design News*, September 2003, http://www.lifeworks-by-design. com/sef/newsletter.html.
7. Gaby Wood, "The Illusionist," *Vogue*, April 1, 2007, 366.
8. "Economics discovers its feelings," *The Economist*, December 19, 2006, 35.
9. Rachel Dupuis, *HR Professional*, August/September, 2005, 44-45.

10. John Blaydes, *The Educator's Book of Quotes* (USA: Corwin Press Inc., 2003). 162.

11. Mac Anderson, "What Are Your Core Values," *Simple Truths*, March 4, 2010.

12. De Angelis, 98.

13. Jim Clemmer, *Leader's Digest* (Canada: TCG Press, 2003), 27–30.

14. Cheryl Richardson, "Graduation: The end is only the beginning," *Life Makeover for the Year 2009*, June 1, 2009.

CHAPTER 2 — Organizational Vision

1. "Sweat and luxury," *The Globe and Mail*, March 30, 2007, 6.

2. Luke De Sadeleer and Joseph Sherren, *Vitamin C for a Healthy Workplace* (Ottawa: Creative Bound, 2001), 66.

3. Anne Greenblatt, "Student handout," *Stanford University*, 2000.

CHAPTER 3 — Personal Leadership

1. Robert Galford and Anne Seibold Drapeau, *The Trusted Leader* (New York: The Free Press, 2002), 30.

2. Harvey Schachter, "The secret to leadership success, I Report on Business," *The Globe and Mail*, August 9, 2010.

3. Justine Menke, *Executive Intelligence: What All Great Leaders Have* (New York: Harper Paperbacks, 2006).

4. Carl Rogers and F. J. Roethlisberger, "Barriers and Gateways to Communication," *Harvard Business Review*, November-December, 1991, 8.

5. Bob Gernon, *Body & Soul: Unleashing the Power of Your Team* (Canada: Detselig Enterprises Ltd., 1999).

6. Tony Alessandra, "Why Don't You Listen to Me! Dr. T's Timely Tips," Issue #110, http://www.alessandra.com/timelytips.

7. Daniel Goleman, Richard Boyatzis and Annie McKee, *Primal Leadership: Learning to Lead with Emotional Intelligence* (Boston: Harvard Business School Press, 2002), 100.
8. Reuven Bar-On and James D.A. Parker, eds., *The Handbook of Emotional Intelligence: Theory, Development, Assessment, and Application at Home, School, and in the Workplace*, (San Francisco: Jossey-Bass, 2000), 322.
9. *Ibid.* 365.
10. Steven J. Stein and Howard E. Book, *The EQ Edge: Emotional Intelligence and our Success*, (Canada: Jossey-Bass, 2006), 206.
11. Goleman, Boyatzis and McKee, *Primal Leadership*, 26.

CHAPTER 4 — Organizational Leadership

1. Warren Bennis, *Managing the Dream: Reflections on Leadership and Change* (New York: Perseus Publishing, 2000), 15.
2. Warren Bennis and Burt Nanus, *Leaders: Strategies for Taking Charge* (New York: Harper Collins, 1985), 85.
3. Robert Eichinger, "Lominger Tools and Services," Korn/Ferry International, *http://www.lominger.com/pdf/Lominger ToolsandServices.pdf*.

CHAPTER 5 — Personal Wellness and Physical-Health Management

1. Carley Sparks, *Aging Smart: Strategies to Live Happier and Healthier Longer* (Canada: Nutrition House, 2006), 14–15.
2. Christiane Northrup, *Women's Bodies, Women's Wisdom: Creating Physical and Emotional Health and Healing* (New York: Bantam Books, 2010), Sony e-Book, chap. 2.
3. Janina Filipczuk (bio-identical hormone expert), in discussion with the author, July 2009.
4. Jillian Michaels, *Master Your Metabolism* (New York: Crown Publishers, 2009), 3.

5. Natasha Turner, *The Hormone Diet: A 3-Step Program to Help You Lose Weight, Gain Strength, and Live Younger Longer* (New York: Rodale Inc., 2009), 311.

6. Joseph Mercola, "Memory Can Be Reversed," *How Does Exercise Protect Your Brain*, February 2, 2010, *http://fitness. mercola.com/sites/fitness/archive/2010/02/02/the-single-most-important-thing-to-preserve-your-brain-function.aspx*.

7. Michael F. Roizen and Mehmet C. Oz, *You are on a Diet – The Owner's Manual for Waist Management* (New York: Free Press, 2006).

8. Jeffrey Rosensweig and Betty Liu, *Age Smart: Discovering the Fountain of Youth at Midlife and Beyond* (New Jersey: Prentice Hall, 2006), 41.

9. Rhonda Rovan, "Move it or Lose it," *CARP Magazine*, October, 2007, 28.

10. Brenda Watson and Leonard Smith, *The Fiber35 Diet: Nature's Weight Loss Secret* (New York: Free Press, 2007), 5.

11. Ibid. 25.

12. Maoshing Ni, *Secrets of Self-Healing: Harness Nature's Power to Heal Common Ailments, Boost Your Vitality, and Achieve Optimum Wellness* (USA: Penguin Group, 2008), 78.

CHAPTER 6 — Personal Wellness and Lifestyle Management

1. Carley Sparks, *Aging Smart*, xxii.

2. Dean Ornish, interview by Larry King, *Larry King Live*, CNN, February 12, 2010.

3. Catherine Price, "Learning to Exhale," *Oprah Magazine*, September, 2010, 246.

4. Dean Ornish, *Love & Survival: The Scientific Basis for the Healing Power of Intimacy* (New York: Harper Collins, 1998), 142 – 144.

5. Kailee Kline (Healthwinds Spa), in discussion with the author, 2009.

6. Lynda Goldman, *How to Make a Million Dollar First Impression* (Canada: GSBC, 2001), 5.
7. Johana Schneider (principal, Dresscode), in discussion with the author, June, 2010.
8. Deepak Chopra, interview by Dr. Mehmet Oz, *The Dr Oz Show*, CTV, March 1, 2010.
9. Leah Zerbe, "Loneliness Is Contagious. Here's How to Stop the Spread," *Rodale News*, December 9, 2009.
10. Melody Beattie, *The Language of Letting Go* (USA: Hazelden, 1990), 218.
11. Ornish, *Love & Survival*, 2.
12. Daniel H. Pink, *A Whole New Mind: Why Right Brainers Will Rule the Future* (New York: Riverhead Books, 2006), 113.
13. Martin Seligman, *Authentic Happiness* (New York: The Free Press, 2002), 249.
14. Holly La Fon, "Live well: Tom Rath explains happiness isn't hard to find if you know where to look," *Success Magazine*, September, 2010.
15. Robin Sharma, *The Greatness Guide: 101 Lessons for Making What's Good at Work and in Life Even Better* (New York: Harper Collins, 2008), 122.
16. Mac Anderson, *The Power of Attitude* (Nashville: J. Countryman, 2004), 70.
17. Robin Sharma, *The Leader Who Had No Title: A Modern Fable on Real Success in Business and Life* (New York: Free Press, 2010), 182 – 183.
18. Robert Kiyosaki, *Rich Dad Poor Dad: What the Rich Teach Their Kids About Money — That the Poor and Middle Class Do Not* (New York: Warner Books, 1998).
19. April Lane Benson, (Ph.D. and author), in discussion with the author, January 2011.
20. Thomas J. Stanley, *The Millionaire Mind* (Kansas City: Andrews McMeel Publishing, 2001), 150.

21. Gail Bebee, *No Hype: The Straight Goods on Investing Your Money* (Toronto: The Ganneth Company, 2008), 17.

22. David Bach, *Smart Women Finish Rich: 9 Steps to Achieving Financial Security and Funding Your Dreams* (New York: Broadway Books, 2002).

23. Dan Richards, "Investors asking tougher questions," *The Globe and Mail*, December 21, 2009, http://www.theglobeandmail.com/globe-investor/investment-ideas/experts-podium/investors-asking-tougher-questions/article1408166/.

24. *Ibid.*

25. Ali Velshi, *Gimme My Money Back: Your Guide to Beating the Financial Crisis* (New York: Sterling and Ross, 2009), 86.

26. Ibid. 87.

27. Bebee, *No Hype*, 186.

Chapter 7 — Organizational Wellness

1. Patrick Lencioni, *The Three Signs of a Miserable Job* (San Francisco: Jossey-Bass, 2007), 12.

BIBLIOGRAPHY

Anderson, Mac. *The Power of Attitude*. Nashville: J. Countryman, 2004.

Bach, David. *Smart Women Finish Rich: 9 Steps to Achieving Financial Security and Funding Your Dreams*. New York: Broadway Books, 2002.

Bar-On, Reuven and James D.A. Parker, eds. *The Handbook of Emotional Intelligence: Theory, Development, Assessment, and Application at Home, School, and in the Workplace*. San Francisco: Jossey-Bass, 2000.

Beattie, Melody. *The Language of Letting Go*. USA: Hazelden, 1990.

Bebee, Gail. *No Hype: The Straight Goods on Investing Your Money*. Toronto: The Ganneth Company, 2008.

Bennis, Warren. *Managing the Dream: Reflections on Leadership and Change*. New York: Perseus Publishing, 2000.

Bennis, Warren and Burt Nanus. *Leaders: Strategies for Taking Charge*. New York: Harper Collins, 1985.

Benson, April Lane. *To Buy or Not to Buy: Why We Overshop and How to Stop*. Boston: Trumpeter, 2008.

Blaydes, John. *The Educator's Book of Quotes*. USA: Corwin Press Inc., 2003.

Clemmer, Jim. *Leader's Digest*. Canada: TCG Press, 2003.

Covey, Stephen. *The 7 Habits of Highly Effective People*. New York: Free Press, 2004.

De Angelis, Barbara. *Real Moments*. New York: Dell Publishing, 1994.

De Sadeleer, Luke and Joseph Sherren. *Vitamin C for a Healthy Workplace*. Ottawa: Creative Bound, 2001.

Galford, Robert and Anne Seibold Drapeau. *The Trusted Leader*. New York: The Free Press, 2002.

Gernon, Bob. *Body & Soul: Unleashing the Power of Your Team*. Canada: Detselig Enterprises Ltd., 1999.

Goldman, Lynda. *How to Make a Million Dollar First Impression*. Canada: GSBC, 2001.

Goleman, Daniel, Richard Boyatzis and Annie McKee. *Primal Leadership: Learning to Lead with Emotional Intelligence*. Boston: Harvard Business School Press, 2002.

Kiyosaki, Robert. *Rich Dad Poor Dad: What the Rich Teach Their Kids About Money — That the Poor and Middle Class Do Not*. New York: Warner Books, 1998.

Klemmer, Brian. *If How-To's Were Enough, We'd All be Skinny, Rich and Happy*. USA: Vision Imprints Publishing, 2005. Audio Book.

Kushner, Harold. *How Good Do We Have to Be?: A New Understanding of Guilt and Forgiveness*. USA: Little, Brown and Company, 2006.

Lencioni, Patrick. *The Three Signs of a Miserable Job*. San Francisco: Jossey-Bass, 2007.

Menke, Justin. *Executive Intelligence: What All Great Leaders Have*. New York: Harper Paperbacks, 2006.

Michaels, Jillian. *Master Your Metabolism*. New York: Crown Publishers, 2009.

Ni, Maoshing. *Secrets of Self-Healing: Harness Nature's Power to Heal Common Ailments, Boost Your Vitality, and Achieve Optimum Wellness*. USA: Penguin Group, 2008.

Northrup, Christiane. *Women's Bodies, Women's Wisdom:*

Creating Physical and Emotional Health and Healing. New York: Bantam Books, 2010.

Ornish, Dean. *Love & Survival: The Scientific Basis for the Healing Power of Intimacy.* New York: Harper Collins, 1998.

Pink, Daniel H. *A Whole New Mind: Why Right Brainers Will Rule the Future.* New York: Riverhead Books, 2006.

Roizen, Michael F. and Mehmet C. Oz. *You On a Diet — The Owner's Manual for Waist Management.* New York: Free Press, 2006.

Rosensweig, Jeffrey and Betty Liu. *Age Smart: Discovering the Fountain of Youth at Midlife and Beyond.* New Jersey: Prentice Hall, 2006.

Rovan, Rhonda. "Move it or Lose it." CARP *Magazine,* October, 2007.

Seligman, Martin. *Authentic Happiness.* New York: The Free Press, 2002.

Sharma, Robin. *The Greatness Guide: 101 Lessons for Making What's Good at Work and in Life Even Better.* New York: Harper Collins, 2008.

Sharma, Robin. *The Leader Who Had No Title: A Modern Fable on Real Success in Business and Life.* New York: Free Press, 2010.

Sparks, Carley. *Aging Smart: Strategies to Live Happier and Healthier Longer.* Canada: Nutrition House, 2006.

Stanley, Thomas J. *The Millionaire Mind.* Kansas City: Andrews McMeel Publishing, 2001.

Stein, Steven J. and Howard E. Book. *The EQ Edge: Emotional Intelligence and our Success.* Canada: Jossey-Bass, 2006.

Turner, Natasha. *The Hormone Diet: A 3-Step Program to Help You Lose Weight, Gain Strength, and Live Younger Longer.* New York: Rodale Inc., 2009.

Velshi, Ali. *Gimme My Money Back: Your Guide to Beating the Financial Crisis.* New York: Sterling and Ross, 2009.

Watson, Brenda and Leonard Smith. *The Fiber35 Diet: Nature's Weight Loss Secret.* New York: Free Press, 2007.

ACKNOWLEDGEMENTS

One of the greatest experiences in writing this book over the past four years has been meeting and working with so many extraordinary and knowledgeable people.

First, thank you to all of those who have used my executive-coaching services over the years whether in leadership development and lifestyle management, consulting in strategic business planning, succession planning, or speaking engagements. My rich work experience with you, as clients, combined with my years of experience as an executive in the corporate sector, has given me the spark and the substance to write *All Together Now*. To my executive coaching clients, thank you for the opportunity to coach you to further discover your own passion, purpose, and vision; to journey with you to a whole new level of leadership; and to have a positive impact on your wellness and lifestyle management to enhance your longevity of life. That's my privilege ... thank you.

Two and a half decades ago, Jack Scott, president of General Foods (now Kraft) along with Richard Peddie, president of one of their major subsidiaries, supported me and several others in the organization to go to night school to study anatomy and physiology and eventually launch the first onsite fitness centre in Toronto. That was the starting point for me as an organizational development specialist to build on integrating vision, leadership, and wellness to coach corporate executives to achieve extraordinary success. Jack and Richard, your support of my work in the early years and over the years is truly what planted the seeds of inspiration for this book.

I am profoundly grateful for the insights of Joan Andersen, a human resources executive and a colleague. She is an expert in my field of organizational development and effectiveness. Her clever and savvy advice, her decisiveness, and her high degree of knowledge in her craft helped shape the fundamental models, theory, and substance of this book.

I am also extremely grateful for the contribution and ongoing commitment of Jacques Guilbault, a highly seasoned professional and organizational leadership consultant. His unique strategic perspective helped make this book relevant to a wide range of corporate executives. Jacques, thank you for keeping me focused on the most important material for the target reader.

My dad has been a constant source of encouragement along this journey. Thank you, Dad, for your relentless belief and confidence in my executive leadership skills and abilities, your patience in discussing the challenges along the way with this book, and your great sense of humour. Your exceptional knowledge of business and finance, along with your high level of integrity in building relationships with clients, has been a treasured source of wisdom and inspiration for me in my own professional pursuits. Thank you, also, Mom for being such a strong woman and for providing me with your unending support throughout my career and always being there for me. Truly, one of the greatest blessings of my life is to have a mother and father like you.

My sister, Theresa Cory, helped organize and articulate much of the information with greater clarity. Thank you for your patience, perseverance, and flexibility over the endless hours of reviewing the draft manuscript and helping to shape the final product.

Dick Cappon, a career transition expert, was a steady source of strength, support, and guidance over the past four years. Dick, your encouragement and insights were fundamental in helping me reach the objective of finishing this book.

I am also thankful to Dr. John C. Marshall, an organizational psychologist, for writing the foreword to the book. I have deep appreciation for his extraordinary expertise, as well as that of Mary Kelly at the Self Management Group.

Input from a variety of medical, health, and fitness practitioners helped me consolidate the most relevant information for corporate executives. I am especially appreciative of the insights of Dr. Stanley J. Wine, Dr. Robert Kingstone, Dr. Terry Ciomyk, Dr. Ken Wolch, Dr. Fred Hui, Janina Filipczuk, and the staff at the Marguerite Bourgeoys Family Centre.

Brenda Melles worked with me for four intensive months in editing my work to prepare the final draft manuscript. Her strong substantive editing skills, along with her value-added expertise in organization development, allowed us to jointly make progress on the draft manuscript in a short timeline.

Thank you Nicole Chaplin, my copy editor at Dundurn Press, for enhancing and finalizing the manuscript and for her enthusiastic support and patient guidance throughout the book-publishing process. Thank you also to Kim Leitch who sought permissions for quotes, Stephanie Casemore, who prepared the index, and Deb Duncan and Lesley Lorimer who provided the graphics services. Thanks also to Glenna Morrison, Deb Duncan, and Sheila Gray who assisted with editing the early versions of this book. I am especially indebted to Nancy Griffin in her outstanding insights and networking ability to connect and match the right people.

I will always be proud of my roots in growing up in the small town of St. Clements, Ontario, Canada, and treasure the support of the community over the years. Most of all, I am grateful for the ever present loving support of my parents, family, friends, relatives, and church. To everyone who has supported and helped me on this journey, I feel privileged and grateful to have you in my life. Every day with you is precious.

INDEX

Page numbers in *italics* indicate a diagram or graphic.

ABOUT THE AUTHOR

Gail Voisin is a world-class executive coach, speaker, educator, author, and expert on executive leadership development, lifestyle management and wellness, succession planning, and strategic business planning. She is the CEO of Gail Voisin Executive Coaching, which she started in 1997, and a trusted advisor to high performers — primarily corporate executives and high potential candidates — around issues of leadership, personal and organizational effectiveness, and wellness.

Her competitive edge is her unique combination of background and skills that define her as an expert in vision, leadership, and wellness. Over the years, she has developed a method that has since become a compelling brand called The All Together Now Advantage.

With 25 years of experience in the consumer packaged goods, retail, high-tech, utilities and energy, broadcasting, sports and entertainment, hospitality, manufacturing, and financial services industries, Gail is one of the first corporate organization development specialists in Canada to design and incorporate health and wellness into core management development programs, connecting the balance of life with increased productivity and return on human assets for the organization.

As a graduate of University of Western Ontario, she holds a bachelor of arts (BA) and has a certified human resources professional designation (CHRP). Gail is a member of the faculty and national coaching team for the Banff Executive Leadership Program. She has studied human anatomy and physiology, taught physical fitness for seven years, and completed extensive research on stress management and work/life balance. She has completed additional courses in organizational behavior, finance, international career transition, and board governance.

She delivers presentations on her areas of expertise to corporations, associations, and universities. Gail also participates in panel discussions and volunteers on non-profit, health, and charity advisory boards. In addition to authoring this book, she has written feature articles for various professional publications, and provides interviews and resource information to the media related to her expertise.

To learn more about how Gail Voisin Executive Coaching can help you and your organization, you can visit her website at *www.GailVoisin.com*.

OF RELATED INTEREST

HOW LEADERS SPEAK
Essential Rules for Engaging and Inspiring Others
by Jim Gray
978-1554887019 / $19.99

Senior executives, professionals, politicians, entrepreneurs, and educators are increasingly being evaluated by how well they speak — how credibly, how naturally, and how enthusiastically. They're being judged on their presentation skills. In today's communication-saturated age, the ability to address others effectively has become the essential mark of a leader. *How Leaders Speak* covers the five keys to speaking like a leader: preparation, certainty, passion, engagement, and commitment. It's a personal handbook for planning and conveying presentations that will engage and inspire others, from overcoming nervousness to handling difficult questions from listeners. The book reveals how to connect like an achiever, whether it's delivering a keynote speech, giving a new business pitch, taking part in a panel discussion, or even participating in a media interview. *How Leaders Speak* — it's about finding the leader in you.

BEFORE YOU SAY YES ...
A Guide to the Pleasures and Pitfalls of Volunteer Boards
by Doreen Pendgracs
978-1554887033 / $19.99

Doreen Pendgracs has sat on various boards of directors for the past twenty-five years. During that time, she has gleaned valuable information that she shares in an easy-to-understand, conversational style for novices and seasoned members alike. Whether you're asked to sit on a trade union board, a non-profit board for a community group or church, a business-focused board of an association or chamber of commerce, or the board of a charitable organization, *Before You Say Yes ...* gives you the inside scoop on what questions to ask and what you need to do before you take the plunge.

What did you think of this book?
Visit www.dundurn.com for reviews, videos, updates, and more!